P9-CDJ-855

THEY MADE AMERICA GREAT

--31 Endearing Legacies Worth Heeding Today--

By Rick Rhodes

THEY MADE AMERICA GREAT

--31 Endearing Legacies Worth Heeding Today--

By Rick Rhodes

Copyright © 2017 by Rick Rhodes

All rights reserved.

No portion of this book may be reproduced or transmitted in any manner, or by any electronic or mechanical means including information storage and retrieval systems with written permission from the publisher.

For information about bulk purchases, please contact Heron Island Guides at: 1-888-459-5992 or email rick@rickrhodes.com.

Manufactured in the United States of America

Published by Heron Island Guides
360 Mt. Oak Avenue NE
St. Petersburg, FL 33702

Fax: 727-527-8287
Phone: 727-459-5992
1-888-459-5992
Web: www.heronislandguides.com

Library of Congress Card Number: 2017-901230

ISBN (13): 978-0-9665866-6-4
ISBN (9): 0-9665866-6-2

920.073 RHO
1923-4148 1/10/2018 WBL
Rhodes, Rick,

They made America great.
<cjg>

CONTENTS

Page

V. INSPIRING SERVICE
   IN DAUNTING TIMES 143

VI. CONTRIBUTING IN A
   BUFFUDDLED WORLD 179

LIST OF PHOTOGRAPHS OR PORTRAITS, AND CREDITS

FRONT COVER: Upper Arc (left to right): Benjamin Franklin, George Marshall, John Quincy Adams (top), Harry Truman and Harriet Tubman
Lower Arc (left to right): Frederick Douglass, Ulysses Grant, Christy Matthewson (bottom), Clara Barton and Joshua Lawrence Chamberlain
BACK COVER: Upper Arc (left to right): Daniel Inouye, Chester Arthur, John Wooden (top), David Crockett, and 'Buck' O'Neil.

INSIDE BOOK:

---

[1]The National Portrait Gallery is part of the Smithsonian Institute in Washington DC

AUTHOR'S NOTE

Why did I research and write this book? Foremost, I am an American. I'm an American long before registering as Democrat, Republican, or Independent. And I have been all three. The idea and the research for this project began one year before the 2016 general election.

Until recently, I have always taken a quiet pride in being American. My positive American sentiments became stronger after I developed a comparative viewpoint after working in a third-world Latin American country for a year and a half. However, the presidential race that ended with the election of the 45th President tested that pride. This project is envisioned as an uplifting antidote to that presidential race.

In all the 58 U.S. presidential elections since George Washington, no election campaign lasted longer, and only a few others split our nation with such rancor. Many voters I met viewed one, or the other, and even both major political candidates disagreeably. Founding Father and first White House occupant John Adams said, "…May none but honest and wise men ever rule under this roof." Many feel one or both frontrunners tested John Adams' wish.

My purpose is not to denigrate one or the other political candidate, but simply to point out that in our nation's relatively short past we have had numerous principled men and women in political life, as well as honorable men and women in other pursuits.

A president or any leader – of a country, a company, a team, or even a small club, **sets a tone** – a good, bad or indifferent tone. The behavior of a leader trickles down to the behavior of many others. Our first Republican President, Abraham Lincoln, sought to bring out the 'Better Angels' in our nature. Conversely, it's quite easy for an American president to stoke-up the 'Darkest Demons' in our nature. Please, let's not forget, besides being a force for good, our country has been capable of doing awful things. America was one of the last countries to rid itself of slavery, and encouraged slavery with the passage of two Fugitive Slaves Laws. Our past treatment of Native Americans has been abysmal. At the start of World War II, a Presidential Executive Order took freedoms away from American citizens of Japanese, German and Italian ancestry.

In his 1961 Inaugural Address, President John F. Kennedy set a high tone, "...And so my fellow Americans, ask not what your country can do for you, ask what you can do for your country." Not quite three years later, in a speech President Kennedy had prepared for the Dallas Trade Mart on November 23, 1963, but sadly wasn't able to deliver because he was assassinated the day before wrote, "We in this country are ...the watchman ...of world freedom. We ask therefore that we may be worthy of our power and responsibility that we may exercise our strength with wisdom and restraint, and that we may achieve ...the ancient vision of peace on earth, goodwill toward men."

Knowing American History served President Kennedy well. During the Cuban Missile Crisis of 1962, President Kennedy and his Soviet counterpart, Premier Nikita Khrushchev, both had the acumen as well as the thickness of skin to behave nobly, by NOT heeding the advice of their war-mongering underlings. That October, our world was spared from plunging into a nuclear holocaust, thanks to the statesmanship of both President Kennedy and Premier Khrushchev.

Fifty-five years since Kennedy's death, after a senseless mass murder, in an Orlando, Florida, nightclub, President Barack Obama again challenged Americans, "We have to decide if that's the kind of country we want to be?" I thought this was a fair question to pose to the American people. During President Ronald Reagan's long political life, he referred to America as that "shining city on a hill." In his 1989 farewell speech, Reagan said, "... it was a tall, proud city built on rocks stronger than oceans, wind-swept, God-blessed, and teeming with people of all kinds living in harmony and peace; a city with free ports that hummed with commerce and creativity. And if there had to be city walls, the walls had doors, and the doors were open to anyone with the will and the heart to get here. That's how I saw it, and see it still."

Except for Native Americans, we as immigrant peoples have inhabited North America for barely four centuries, a short time compared to other world civilizations. Nevertheless, within the past 250 years, numerous personal examples of our historical richness abound. All it takes is looking into our nation's rearview mirror, to find Americans who uplift us. My endeavor in this book is to uncover some of these people, and inspire you with their heartwarming and endearing lives.

Looking into our historic rearview mirror, we should be able to grasp what we Americans have done well, and not so well. We should recognize what we did right, and what we did wrong, and learn from both. Apple Computer Cofounder Steve Jobs looked backward for his queues how to move his company forward saying, "You can't connect the dots looking forward; you can only connect them looking backwards. So you have to trust the dots will somehow connect in your future."

For more than a century, American leadership helped stabilize the world. I'm fearful this era of American leadership may be ending. This need not be. If more Americans better understood their history and our nation's place in the world, our possible wane in world leadership could be averted. Not knowing our history could be our national undoing.

Thomas Jefferson, our third president, said, "If a nation expects to be ignorant and free … it expects what never was and never will be." Studying American History, warts and all, is an important and worthwhile endeavor. Clarence Darrow stated, "One of the things wrong with history is that it repeats itself." More recently, Gettysburg College Professor, Allen Guelzo stated, "History, if anything, teaches us humility."

The Greek philosopher Plato, who lived about 2,400 years ago, had profound insights into human nature, which are apropos today. Plato said, "Tyranny naturally arises out of democracy; the tyrant first appears as a protector; and tyranny is always better organized than freedom." Lest we forget. As a child, I recall my well-read father, and a World War II veteran, telling me America was, and would always be, too strong to fall to foreign powers; but our country's demise would likely come from within.

Using the lens of American history, we should be able to reach conclusions on certain subjects. For example, President Lincoln was faced with a horrible dilemma. He took action, much of it unpopular, but he left our country on sounder moral footing, albeit at a horrific cost, our Civil War.

In today's America, anybody can spread fake news. Partially fabricated news is the worst offense. In today's America, countless *legitimate* looking websites are in the business of spreading lies and defaming public figures, most of whom are still alive. The harm done and the money made spreading fake news are immense. 'Alternative facts' is an oxymoron. Matt Brown of Tampa, Florida's ABC News Affiliate said when 'facts' confront 'beliefs,' people invariably chose their more comforting beliefs over solid facts pointing in an opposite direction. Similarly, opinions, no matter how madcap they are, cannot really be considered wrong.

Today, anybody can write a book. Researching for it well is another matter. However, when researching people and events from our past, as in this book, it is more difficult to distort facts. I hope the researched and documented events from our shared national past, presented here, will help you, a reader facing a glut of news and jaded by fake news.

It's the rage today to demonize or attempt to destroy the opposition. When an opposition's shortcomings become obvious, the opponent turns downright gleeful. Media pundits promote this behavior. This is the equivalent of rubbing your defeated adversary's nose in the dirt. That will only come back to haunt. None of the past great Americans in this book acted in this way. General Joshua Lawrence Chamberlain set a clear and noble example of what should make all Americans proud.

We Americans should know who went before us, and how we arrived at this place in time. Some of the folks found inside these pages are politicians, but many are not. This project is my effort to unearth great Americans, and share a small portion of their lives with you.

Having previously researched and written nine nonfiction boating guidebooks, I have developed a special kinship for regional and national history. I cannot get enough of it. I also desire to share this. The result of that passion is this work.

Today, where is that 'Shining City on a Hill?' Where can we find the 'Better Angels in our nature?' They are there. But we have to find them by looking backwards into our nation's rearview mirror. This book is my effort to share these 'better angels' with you.

Rick Rhodes

INTRODUCTION

Our American Experience is mixed. At times, it is poignant; heartbreaking, and even shameful. This work assembles 31 real-life heart-warming stories of Americans who helped forge our national identity – for the better. Although all of them are departed, their actions live on.

While researching and crafting these summaries, there was no conscious plan to connect the 31 pieces. However, in a handful of instances, the logic became apparent. For example, George Rogers Clark connected to Meriwether Lewis, Albert Gallatin to Meriwether Lewis, Albert Gallatin to John Quincy Adams, Harriet Tubman to Frederick Douglass, Harriet Tubman to William Henry Seward, Ulysses S. Grant to Joshua Lawrence Chamberlain, Clara Barton to Chester Arthur, George Marshall to Harry Truman, and even Benjamin Franklin to the 9-11 First Responders.

The word inspire may be trite. However, as you read through these 31 pieces, something may inspire you. Hopefully, you will be touched by that small beacon of light, shinning from behind, illuminating the path we Americans have already taken.

Thirty-one stories of Americans from different walks of life are presented. Some people are famous, while other are much lesser known. Yet they all contributed to our indelible American Legacy. Not all aspects of their lives are addressed. Much longer, well-researched books do this in more detail. For this project, this author read and listened to those numerous sources, and distilled highlights for you. This hopefully makes more straightforward reading for one accustomed to receiving news via sound bites, short news clips, and constant news barrages from CNN, and the like.

Our 31 legacies are divided into six chronological eras: 1) 'American Frontiersmen,' 2) 'When Right and Wrong Were Blurred,' 3) 'Civil War Luminaries,' 4) 'American Growing Pains and Baseball,' 5) 'Inspiring Service in Daunting Times,' and 6) 'Contributing in a Befuddled World.' Naturally, there was some overlap. A legacy is placed where it fits best, usually within the timeframe of our legacy's greatest contribution to our American experience.

No doubt there are thousands of other Americans worthy of this book. Those few mentioned here are some of this author's personal favorites — David Crockett, Harriet Tubman, Ulysses S. Grant, and Harry Truman. The 'THEY' in this book are, by far, not the only ones who 'Made America Great.' But this author believes that the 'They' represents a cross-section of us all. Two personal favorites, Abraham Lincoln and Mark Twain, have no dedicated chapter in this book. This is not because they are held in lesser regard. Their stories should already be widely known. The reader will find President Lincoln's contributions to America woven into many other personalities in this book. Besides Lincoln, the other three great presidents on Mount Rushmore are also not addressed in a dedicated chapter.

This work begins with Founding Father Benjamin Franklin. He was a genius, yet he was born into the working class. Throughout our world of billions, undoubtedly there are many geniuses born. Most are born poor and never heard from. But Benjamin Franklin was born in Colonial America when the sprouts of individual effort were taking hold. A youthful Franklin realized this, and grabbed onto the rungs ...and the rest is history.

Benjamin Franklin

I.   AMERICAN FRONTIERSMEN

1

Benjamin Franklin (1706-1790)

...Common Sense Realist and Compromiser

In May of 1787, four years after America won independence from Great Britain our country had a dangerously weak central government, one that couldn't even collect taxes.   Operating under the Articles of Confederation, it was obvious the union in America would dissolve if these Articles of Confederation were not changed or replaced with something better.

Fifty-five delegates representing 12 of the 13 states met during a steamy summer in Philadelphia's Independence Hall.   Virginia's George Washington was unanimously elected to preside over this convention. Benjamin Franklin, the oldest framer, was one of the eight delegates from Pennsylvania. After more than three and a half months of arguing, debating, posturing, and negotiating, there was still resistance because of differences over issues.   These issues included slavery, the amount of power held by the central government, and how to handle impending disputes between states.

From the first day of that 1787 Constitutional Convention, Benjamin Franklin was the strongest voice for compromise. Franklin implored the assembly to part with some of their individual demands. He promoted and furthered the idea of two houses of Congress. This helped address the issue of adequate representation between smaller and larger states in a centralized government.

On September 17, 1787, the last day of the convention, 81-year old Benjamin Franklin gave an eloquent speech, "Mr. President, I confess that there are several parts of this constitution which I do not at present approve …For having lived long, I have experienced many instances of being obliged by better information …to change opinions even on important subjects, which I once thought right …It is therefore that the older I grow, the more apt I am to doubt my own judgment, and to pay more respect to the judgment of others. Most men indeed, as well as most sects in religion, think themselves in possession of all truth …In these sentiments, Sir, I agree to this Constitution with all its faults …For when you assemble a number of men to have the advantage of their joint wisdom, you inevitably assemble with those men, all their prejudices, their passions …and their selfish views. From such an assembly can a perfect production be expected? …Thus I consent, Sir, to this Constitution because I expect no better, and because I am not sure, that it is not the best …I hope therefore that for our own sakes …and for the sake of posterity, we shall act heartily and unanimously in recommending this Constitution …On the whole, Sir, I cannot help expressing a wish that every member of the Convention who may still have objections to it, would with me, on this occasion, doubt a little of his own infallibility and …put his name to this instrument."

Thirty-nine of the 55 Philadelphia delegates signed our Constitution; but it still had to be ratified by at least nine of the states. Franklin was pleased, and in his own words, "Let the Experiment [of the United States] Run!"

Three-quarters of a century after Benjamin Franklin's profound advice on compromise, during the horrific Civil War, our 16th President Abraham Lincoln expounded, "In great contests each party claims to act in accordance with the will of God. **Both may be**, and one must be, **wrong**, for God cannot be for and against the same thing at the same time."

Benjamin Franklin was the only Founding Father to sign all three – the U.S. Constitution, the Peace Treaty with England, and the Declaration of Independence. Most of our Declaration of Independence was drafted by Thomas Jefferson, but Benjamin Franklin crafted a few thoughtful edits, including changing Jefferson's wording from: "We hold these truths to be **sacred and undeniable**…" to "We hold these truths to be **self-evident**…"

Benjamin Franklin, one of the greatest homegrown thinkers, was the most multi-faceted Founding Father. He was a humorous man, and found laughter in many things.[2] Late in his long life, he believed the best advice he gave was 'compromise.' Ben Franklin exemplified tolerance and at least paying attention to opposing views. During that 1787 Convention, Franklin urged his fellow delegates to be willing to sacrifice, not their principles, but their overwhelming urge to be right. It's certain Benjamin Franklin would offer his fellow citizens this same advice today.

Benjamin Franklin, who graces our $100 bill, came from humble beginnings. His father, Josiah, was a Boston soap and candle-maker. Josiah had many children, four by his first wife, and ten by his second wife, Abiah Folger. Benjamin was Josiah's youngest son.[3] Josiah attempted to prepare young Benjamin for the clergy. That didn't well suit Ben as he was insatiably curious about so many other things.

Young Ben borrowed and read many books. He taught himself arithmetic, grammar, and philosophy. At a time when few people could swim, Ben even taught himself to swim by first reading a 'how-to' book on swimming.

Ben was apprenticed to his older brother James' print shop. Capable 16-year old Ben, while working in his brother's shop, wrote his first series of stories. Ben secretly authored *'Silence Dogood,'* a supposedly middle-aged widow. Her name appeared on witty and satirical contributions found at James' print shop door. James found success in printing the stories of *'Silence Dogood'* as a series in his *New England Courant.* When James eventually learned the author of *'Silence Dogood'* was his younger brother Ben, he became envious and mistreated Ben. Ben broke his apprenticeship and fled south. After arriving in New York by ship, Benjamin wearily trudged across New Jersey.[4] At seventeen years old he arrived in Philadelphia an impoverished runaway.

Before long, quick-study Benjamin found print shop work. Ben soon impressed the royal governor of Pennsylvania. The governor helped Ben further his print shop ambitions by arranging a sailing trip to London. Hanging out in the London coffeehouses, Ben noticed radical ideas were bubbling up and debated during this 'Age of Enlightenment.'

Ben loved this exchange of ideas, many of which countered the established thinking of the day. For example: a poor person need not be condemned to poverty forever. With education and industry, one could greatly improve his station in life. In 1726, at twenty years old, and after being stimulated by London society, Ben sailed back to Philadelphia determined to make something more of his life.

After returning to Philadelphia, Ben was back in business with his own print-shop. In his *Pennsylvania Gazette*, Ben saw selling the news akin to selling entertainment. Many considered the *Pennsylvania Gazette* our first national newspaper. When his newspaper press was idle, Franklin devised and published *Poor Richard's Almanac*. *Poor Richard's Almanac* was loaded with profound sayings, and offered practical advice on how to get along in the world. It was a sellout for 25 years.

In 1730, Benjamin had an out of wedlock son, William. Later that same year, Benjamin married long-time friend Deborah Read. Deborah's affections toward little William were questionable, at best. Later, Ben and Deborah had two more children. Sadly, Ben's second son, Francis, succumbed to smallpox at four years old. Their daughter, Sarah, survived well into adulthood.

By 1741 at age 42, Benjamin Franklin had become a wealthy Philadelphia printer, and soon retired from business. But wealth was not his end game. Franklin felt grateful to Pennsylvania for the chance to rise from poverty.[5] Yet he saw no point in continuing to simply pile-up money. He called it the pursuit of wealth without purpose.[6] Rather, Franklin longed to expand his horizons and unleash his imaginative inventiveness. Franklin knew real success lay in 'giving back' to his community.

Franklin joined a liked-minded group of fellow Philadelphia businessmen who called themselves the 'Junto.' The 12-member Junto's meetings, often lubricated with alcohol, promoted small community improvements that made life easier for ordinary people. Today, the Junto might be akin to a local Rotary Club.

Franklin and his Junto set up the first lending book library in America. He helped found the Pennsylvania Hospital and the Philadelphia Academy, the first non-religious college in America. That institution survives today as the University of Pennsylvania. Ben Franklin believed all religions had a potential for good, but he himself cared little about religious dogma and rigidity. He believed entry into heaven ought not be bound by predestination, but rather on the good done in this life.

Franklin's active mind was a treasure chest of new ideas. He streamlined the inefficient Philadelphia Post Office, making it profitable for the very first time. He even studied storm clouds and the social behavior of ants. He had the rather radical ideas for a union in the North American British Colonies. Franklin was one of the few who thought in terms of an entire continent, versus his specific colony.

In his passion for science, he wondered how lightening energy in storm clouds could serve humanity. In about 1750, he developed the Franklin Rod, a lightening-grounding device, still used today as a reliable method to channel lightening from that destructive bolt harmlessly into the ground.

In his experiments with lightening, some clergymen saw Franklin as overstepping God. In those days, if a house was hit by lightening and began to burn, many in the clergy saw it simply as 'God's Will.' The local fire-fighting brigade attempted to extinguish the spreading fires to nearby dwellings, but the brigade would let the struck house burn down, since this was God's Will. Franklin countered the clergy, noting that just putting a roof on a house to protect it from rain and hail amounted to the same thing ...that is, to protect the house from the 'forces of nature,' versus from the 'wrath of an angry God.'

Franklin also developed the efficient Franklin Stove. This stove stood in the middle of a room, versus along an outside brick wall, and had a series of baffles capable of circulating hot air better than a fireplace. Franklin didn't earn a dime from either the stove or the lightening rod, because he didn't patent them. He considered these contributions to the well-being of society. He just didn't need more money.

Even later in life, Franklin's inquisitive mind never rested. While a diplomat in France, he studied hail storms and conceived the idea of bi-focal eyeglasses. He also concocted the idea of Daylight Savings Time. Rather than the predatory bald eagle as our national emblem, Ben Franklin suggested the less assuming turkey.

In 1757, Franklin, and his son William, sailed to England. The elder Franklin was now a well-known scientist and public figure. His primary mission was to lobby against the interests of the powerful Penn family of Pennsylvania. The younger William was especially enamored with London's high society. William was soon offered the appointment of Royal Governor of New Jersey. While in England, William Franklin fathered an out of wedlock son – Temple Franklin. Like father, like son.

During most of his adult life, Benjamin Franklin prided himself as being a cultured Englishman, rather than an upstart American. He believed being a British subject was the best thing going. But in time, he divorced himself as an Englishman.

In 1764, Benjamin Franklin again sailed for London. The British, seeking a revenue source after incurring debts from the Colonists' French and Indian War, sought to increase their colonies' taxes. The Stamp Act of 1765 imposed a tax on all printed materials such as newspapers, contracts, marriage licenses, and wills consumed by their American Colonies. Many colonists vehemently opposed the Stamp Act and sometimes resorted to mob violence. Franklin was less opposed to it than many of his fellow colonists. Nevertheless, in 1766, Franklin was instrumental in getting the Stamp Act repealed. This did not endear him to many aristocrats in London. Tensions between Britain and the colonies remained high.

Franklin also visited the impoverished British Colony in Ireland. He didn't like what he saw. Franklin was fearful British pride and greed affected the American Colonies in the same way these elements had adversely affected Ireland.

Over time, besides Pennsylvania, Franklin was representing more colonies in their grievances against the Crown, including the biggest firebrand colony, Massachusetts. Anybody representing Massachusetts was likely to be unpopular in Britain.

Two years after the Stamp Act, another set of British revenue enhancing measures was imposed upon the Colonists, the Townshend Acts. The Townshend Acts imposed heavy duties on paper, lead, glass, and other commodities the Colonists imported from England. The Townshend Acts were eventually repealed, except for one small tax on tea. That tax lead to the famous Boston Tea Party. In 1773, Colonist disguised as

Mohawk Indians pillaged and dumped more than 300 tea chests into Boston Harbor. The Colonial pillagers asserted it was less about destroying the individual tea chests, but more about 'No taxation without representation.'

Trying to diffuse even more tension between the Colonies and the Crown, Franklin leaked an incriminating letter back to the colonies, hoping the colonists would redirect their anger from London, to one 'bad apple' – the hard-lined Colonial Governor in Massachusetts. This ploy backfired. Instead of the Massachusetts Royal Governor being the scapegoat, Benjamin Franklin was targeted the scapegoat.

When London discovered Franklin's ruse, he was summoned before a British court and branded an incendiary. He had to defend himself for leaking this letter, and was severely dressed down. A proud British subject for 70 years, now badly humiliated, Franklin became committed to the American independence cause. He was no longer the pacifier. But his son, William, remained steadfastly allied with the British. In 1782, son William Franklin permanently departed America to live the rest of his life in Britain.

In 1775, when Benjamin departed London for Philadelphia, his grandson Temple accompanied his grandfather to the colonies. Benjamin had also learned his wife, Deborah, had recently passed away. Nevertheless, during that westward sailing journey, the always-inquisitive Franklin pondered why it took a sailing ship several weeks longer to sail from east-to-west than from west-to-east, basically traversing the same route. From his vessel, dipping a container tied to rope, he found unusually warm water. Ben Franklin discovered the Gulf Stream, that westward moving river of warm water within the Atlantic Ocean that originates in the Gulf of Mexico. The Gulf Stream keeps the winters of Northern Europe relatively mild.

On July 4, 1776, the Colonists declared their Independence from England. Benjamin Franklin was one of the fifty-six signers to that document. Years of war would ensue. The outcome remained uncertain. The fate of the signers, should they lose their cause, would likely be death. Responding to John Hancock's comment about being hanged together should they lose the cause, Franklin replied, "Yes, we must, indeed, all hang together, or most assuredly we shall all hang separately."

Early in the Revolutionary War, things looked badly for the colonists. It appeared son, William Franklin, was correct in assessing the colonists had next-to-no chance against Britain's professional army and navy. Nevertheless, in the fall of 1776, Benjamin Franklin set sail across the Atlantic once again, this time looking for a dearly needed American ally in France. Franklin's only surviving sister tried to dissuade her 70-year brother, and believed this new America had little chance to succeed.

Franklin believed America's effort had little chance without help from the French, Britain's most powerful enemy. Thirteen years earlier, France was defeated by the British during the French and Indian War. Nevertheless, France was naturally wary about entering another losing cause and lending money to the bankrupt Americans. Would King Louis XVI bankroll the American cause? Would our new country's first ambassador, Benjamin Franklin, have any success?

Getting France involved was no small task. France was run by a king. The French aristocracy was uncomfortable, to say the least, hearing local talk about 'unshackling from a king.' When Franklin arrived in Paris, the city was beset with many problems. The rich partook in a life of opulence, while most residents lived in squalor. Franklin's mastery of the French language was poor. But Franklin's accumulated life skills proved invaluable and something a younger colleague, even with more energy, could not live up to. Franklin did an incredible amount of work while in France.

As it turned out, Franklin enthralled the French aristocracy. The nobility took a liking to this private citizen, with a colorfully rustic message. Franklin wore a coonskin hat and successfully played-up to the Quaker American frontiersman's image of which he was neither. He easily adapted to French social whims and became skillful at playing politics, 'French style.'

Franklin had his critiques back in America, mostly out of jealousy. By the fall of 1777, the news from America had all been worrisome. In those days, it took about one month for news to travel across the Atlantic. Why should the French jump in? There was nothing for France to gain? The first good news came after the American victory at Saratoga, New York, in October 1777. In February 1778, the French signed an alliance with the upstart Americans. In March 1778, France became the first country to formally recognize American Independence, and no longer British Colonies. France also sent gunpowder and a young General, Marquis de Lafayette, to America.

In 1778, humorless John Adams joined the American delegation in Paris. John Adams didn't possess Franklin's delicacy and like 'a bull in a china shop,' was hampering Franklin's diplomacy. Franklin flattered the French and made progress. But the Puritanical John Adams often offended his French hosts. John Adams would be up and working by 8:00 AM, but Franklin was able to make much more headway in the French parlors schmoozing at 2:00 A.M.

After about a year in France, Adams was relieved and the full weight of the mission fell on Benjamin Franklin's shoulders. Franklin was worn-out, and asked the American government to relieve him, too. The government wisely dared not to, because they realized how much they needed Franklin in his efforts working with the French. When Franklin was NOT relieved, he felt vindicated.

In September 1781, the French Navy was victorious over the British Navy at the 'Battle of the Capes,' off the mouth of the Chesapeake Bay. With that loss, the British Navy was unable to reinforce or evacuate General Charles Cornwallis' Army encamped off Virginia's York River. One month later, isolated British General Cornwallis surrendered to American General George Washington at Yorktown, Virginia. Two years after the victory at Yorktown, hostilities between America and Britain ceased. After America won its independence from Britain, it behooved both Britain and France to become allies with our young country.

In the subsequent years, during peace negotiations with Britain, John Adams and John Jay sidelined France. Benjamin Franklin was again placed in an embarrassing position, this time with the friends he had cultivated during his years in France. France was slighted, and Franklin felt horrible.

Due to the Treaty of Paris, Franklin knew America would someday need land west of the original colonies, all of the way to the Mississippi River, in order to expand. Franklin insisted America not give-away the rights of Mississippi River navigation to European powers. Within a dozen years, four nations would be lusting for that Mississippi River. Thanks to Benjamin Franklin, our young nation was well poised to take the best advantage of this river.

In 1785, when 79-year old Benjamin Franklin finally returned to America, Philadelphia was the new nation's capitol. As an old man, Franklin took a public stand against slavery. He was the president of America's first abolitionist society. Ahead of many in his day, Franklin believed in women's education. Franklin realized a **learned** middle-class was needed to keep our democracy alive. He was willing to change his convictions based on observation. Franklin championed tolerance, compromise and human reason. He knew compromise was not a sign of weakness.

In the closing days of that 1787 Philadelphia Convention, Benjamin Franklin, tried to persuade both sides to compromise from their steadfast positions. He made this point, "When a broad table is to be made, and the edges of planks do not fit, the artist takes a little from both, and makes a good joint. In like manner here, both sides must part with some of their demands."

In 1790, for this great man's funeral, thirty-four preachers, priests and rabbis marched arm in arm to pay their respects. The epitaph on his tomb reads, "Benjamin Franklin, Printer." He took pride in being a tradesman – a printer. President Harry Truman said, "Franklin has not yet found his place in American history." Why not follow Franklin's example, and learn how to compromise among ourselves, and with the rest of the world. Above all, by following Benjamin Franklin's example, we will remain devoted to his ideal of America as a nation of free people.

SOURCES:
Bridgers, Raymond, *'Benjamin Franklin –The History Channel,'* 2004
Fleming, Thomas, *'Ben Franklin –Inventing America,'* Four Winds
	Press/Quartro Publishing Group, Minneapolis, MN, 1973
Hovde, Ellen and Meyer, Muffie, *'Benjamin Franklin –An extraordinary
	Life, and Electric Mind,'* DVD, Twin Cities Public TV; St. Paul, MN, 2002

2

George Rogers Clark (1752-1818)

...Boldness Winning the Revolutionary West

People often view the Revolutionary War (1775-83) as being fought and won in the east. That's not totally true. What about those western regions, now Kentucky, Ohio, Indiana, and Illinois? The revolution could have easily been lost in the west, were it not for one great leader and soldier, George Rogers Clark. Clark was known for leading his 'Kentucky Long Knives' or 'Big Knives,' in the west during the American Revolution. Clark's men were vastly outnumbered by British-allied Native Americans. More often than not, Clark had fewer than 200 men.

George Rogers Clark had a broad strategic vision not tied to a single location or state. Clark marshaled the scant resources available in the west, while obtaining some government help from the east.[7] Clark knew success meant carrying the war to the enemy rather than remaining in a defensive posture. Clark understood psychology and had an instinct for diplomacy when it came to dealing with French settlers as well as when confronting adversarial Native Americans.[8]

George Rogers Clark was born close to the home of fellow Virginian, Thomas Jefferson. Five of the six Clark boys served as officers during the American Revolution but William Clark was too young to serve. Nevertheless, William Clark co-led the famous Corps of Discovery.

George Rogers Clark's military career began in 1774 during Lord Dunmore's War, a short precursor conflict before the American Revolution. During Lord Dunmore's War, Clark realized he had a gift for command and he learned military structure. He also familiarized himself with Native American ways. After that war, George Rogers Clark spent months surveying in Kentucky, and falling in love with this western country. Clark planned to make surveying in Kentucky his career.[9] He decided to help turn Kentucky into a county of Virginia.

George Rogers Clark

In 1776, the local Kentucky militia had selected Major George Rogers Clark to deliver a petition to Virginia Governor Patrick Henry, asking Virginia to extend its western boundary to include the new 'Kentucky County.' Clark saw the need to acquire gunpowder to defend those western Virginia buffer settlements located in 'Kentucky County.' He believed the very survival of Kentucky County necessitated taking the offensive and carrying the war into enemy territory.[10] Hence, George Rogers Clark and Governor Patrick Henry concocted a plan to capture the British-held villages in the Illinois Country, at Kaskaskia, Prairie du Rocher, St. Phillips, Cahokia, and Vincennes. At that time, the Illinois Country included both Illinois and Indiana. Patrick Henry and Clark agreed they needed the element of surprise to take these forts.

Besides needing to take-out about a half-dozen small British outpost, Clark's men had to potentially combat hundreds, if not thousands, of Native Americans ...or they would fail. At the start of our Revolutionary War, most, but not all, of the Native Americans had allied themselves with the British and for good reason. Generally, Native Americans believed that with a British victory the Crown would keep westward expansion of their upstart colonies in check.

Eager colonial settlers often purchased Native American Lands from dishonest holding companies that had no right to this land in the first place. When the unsuspecting settlers moved onto and began cultivating these Native American Lands, the local Native Americans were justifiably outraged. Misunderstanding and bloodshed typically followed.

The many Native Americans could easily wipe out Clark's tiny American contingent. Clark needed to either neutralize or win over Native Americans. He adeptly used psychology to do this. He often asked the chiefs of a large group of gathered Native American to choose one of two symbolic belts. One belt represented war with the Americans, and if they chose this war belt, he asked them to fight like the brave warriors they were. Or, they could choose the other belt, which represented peace with the Americans. This symbol-laden bluff invariably worked the way Clark had hoped.

From Fort Pitt, at the Forks of the Ohio, Clark's 'Kentucky Big Knives' took flatboats to Corn Island on the Ohio River, near present-day Louisville. During the summer of 1778, Clark and about 175 men crossed the Ohio River from western Kentucky into Illinois at the remains of an old French fort, Fort Massac. Afterward, rather than taking the more obvious river route, Clark marched his men overland in Illinois to the village of Kaskaskia, on the Mississippi River. Approaching Kaskaskia, Clark learned there were no British soldiers there, or in the nearby town of Cahokia. The small French militia in town had no reason to fight the Americans.[11]

Nearing Kaskaskia, Clark's men obtained some boats and used them to cross the last river. On the night of July 4, 1778, Clark's men took the village of Kaskaskia without firing a shot. Within days, Clark's men easily took the three villages north of Kaskaskia, including Cahokia. Within two months, Clark's forces also took the town of Vincennes on the Wabash River, 150 miles to the east.

The French inhabitants of these villages were slow to take up arms against the Americans. They held unpleasant memories of losing the French and Indian War to the British fifteen years prior. Frenchmen were not enamored with British rule. Nonetheless, the French had been conditioned by the British to fear the worst from the savage Americans. Initially Clark did nothing to dispel this fear. But Clark knew he needed the support of French villagers. In time, Clark showed understanding and compassion towards the French. The French villagers were pleased when Clark turned out to be a fair and just military leader, even settling squabbles among the French, themselves. Before long, he won over their hearts and minds.

Native Americans needed little encouragement to resent and attack white American intruders settling on their lands. Nonetheless, Clark was skilled in understanding Native Americans perceptions. He learned this during Lord Dunmore's War. George Rogers Clark knew how to impress and win over Native Americans with his aloof and confident demeanor. He employed a psychological mix of straight-shooting negotiations, toughness, and compassion.

When a group of Paun Indians unsuccessfully tried to sneak into his camp, the Pauns were caught and captured. Two Paun Chiefs tried to back-peddle, offering Clark a peace pipe. Clark smashed the pipe with his sword, and called them old squaws. One could have cut the air with a knife. Then, two young Paun warriors offered themselves to be sacrificed for this guilty act by their tribe. After a prolonged silence, Clark praised the two warriors for their courage, and granted peace and friendship to all their people. Many other Native Americans were favorably impressed with this young Big Knife. George Rogers Clark spoke and acted like no other white man ever had.

Clark concluded no less than ten peace treaties with Native Americans. Author Dale Van Every stated, "The great achievement of Clark's 1778 Campaign was not the uncontested occupation of the Illinois [territory], but his success in neutralizing so considerable a segment of the Indian military power upon which English strategy had depended." Clark *talked the talk*, but he also *walked the walk*.

After his successes in southwestern Illinois, Clark learned Vincennes and its fort, Fort Sackville about 150 miles to their east, were retaken by British forces during Christmas week of 1778. The British commander at Vincennes was waiting until springtime to mount an assault on Kaskaskia and the other villages Clark had recently taken. Upon learning the British had retaken Vincennes, Clark devised a plan of his own. Clark would NOT wait until springtime. During the winter of 1778-79, Clark's force of about 170 would march eastward through the swamps of southern Illinois, and surprise attack the British and recapture Vincennes.

Clark's fair treatment of the French also paid-off. Father Gibault, the local priest and community leader in Kaskaskia, noticed how fairly Clark treated his fellow Frenchmen. Gibault turned out to be a great ally of Clark. Father Gibault made a reconnaissance trip to Vincennes and reported back to Clark the French citizenry in Vincennes, should the Americans march there, would not take up arms against the Americans. Later, many Frenchmen from Kaskaskia also marched alongside Clark to Vincennes.

In February 1779, when Clark and his men reached the Little Wabash River, about 40 miles from Vincennes, the snow-melt had created a sheet of water, sometimes three or four feet deep. Clark's men had to wade through this icy water for miles and miles, in some places chest-high. With Clark's leadership, they overcame this obstacle. When they reached the deeper Wabash River, Clark's men built canoes to ferry themselves across the river.

Nearing Vincennes, Clark captured a local duck hunter. The hunter told Clark the British in Fort Sackville were unaware of the nearby Americans. Clark was also able to reaffirmed the French citizens would remain neutral in an impending battle between the British and the Americans. However, Clark learned there were about 200 British allied Native Americans nearby.

When in sight of Vincennes, but not in sight of Fort Sackville, Clark paraded his men back and forth. Falling for Clark's ruse, the French citizenry in Vincennes reported to the commander at Fort Sackville, the American force was quite large, much larger than, in fact, it actually was. Clark called for the commander of Fort Sackville to surrender.

British-held Fort Sackville was defended by about 80 men, and it could have, at worst, held-off Clark's 170 men for a good while. Nevertheless, Clark met with the British commander, bluffed about the strength of his forces, and persuaded the British commander to surrender. The British commander did not call Clark's bluff. He surrendered.

Vincennes was retaken by the Americans without losing a soldier. Through the force of Clark's personality and his leadership, he had accomplished with surprisingly little bloodshed a feat – the taking of Vincennes and Fort Sackville – that most military commanders would have rejected as impossible.[12]

In October 1781, General Cornwallis surrendered his British army at Yorktown. The Revolutionary War in the east was almost at an end. Nevertheless, events in the east had little impact on the war in the west. For years to come, the British would hold other western forts, like Detroit. The British continued to supply Native Americans with weapons and goods.[13] The year, 1782, would be a most treacherous time for western Revolutionary War fighters, including George Rogers Clark.

In August 1782, Native Americans, prompted by the British, had tricked about 180 Kentuckians into following them into an ambush at Blue Licks, Kentucky. Over one-third of the Kentuckians were lost. George Rogers Clark, their undisputed leader, was not present at this ambush, but he was blamed for the massacre. Following the Blue Licks ambush, Clark led a punitive expedition into Ohio, destroying Native American villages along the Great Miami River. This was one of the last major expeditions of the Revolutionary War.

George Rogers Clark was barely thirty years old when the Revolutionary War ended. His great military achievements were behind him. In the 1783 *Treaty of Paris*, the British ceded the entire Northwest Territory to the United States, and George Rogers Clark was hailed as the 'Conqueror of the Northwest.'

George Rogers Clark knew how to play upon the imaginations, fears and emotions of his adversaries. His reputation remained higher among the Native Americans than with his own peers in Kentucky and Virginia. George Rogers Clark has been rightfully anointed 'The Savior of Kentucky.'

Clark lived too long for the good of his reputation.[14] His major military successes took place before he was thirty years old. Clark was reasonably wealthy at the onset of the Revolutionary War, but by the end of the war, he was deeply in debt. Clark used his own resources and borrowed from friends to continue his campaigns after the funds from Virginia dried up. Virginia never fully repaid him for personal wartime expenses.

Indebted, Clark found solace in whiskey. After suffering a stroke and having a leg amputated, he became an invalid. Clark remained depressed. His happiest moment came in November 1806, when his younger brother William Clark, along with Meriwether Lewis, stopped for a visit soon after completing their successful and historic Corps of Discovery mission to the Pacific Northwest.[15]

SOURCES:
DeLeeuw, Adele, *'George Rogers Clark – Frontier Fighter,'* Garrard
    Publishing Company, Champaign, IL, 1967
Harrison, Lowell H., *'George Rogers Clark and the War in the West,'*
    University of Kentucky Press, Lexington, KY, 1976
Lee, Susan and John, *'George Rogers Clark: War in West,'* Regensteiner
    Publishing Inc., Chicago, IL, 1975

3

Albert Gallatin (1761-1849)

...He Adopted America, and Became our Treasure

Albert Gallatin was born in Europe's French-speaking Geneva. In 1780, Gallatin and another young Genevan left their upper-class European comforts and boldly sailed for America. They dreamed of being land barons in the unknown American western frontier. In 1785, Gallatin became an American citizen by swearing allegiance to the Commonwealth of Virginia.[16]

Gallatin served brilliantly as a statesman, diplomat and financier. He helped bring the War of 1812 to a close and contributed to America's collaborative relationships with France, Great Britain, Netherlands and Canada. Unlike his contemporaries, Aaron Burr and Alexander Hamilton, Gallatin's reputation was handicapped by his exemplary fine character. Unlike many public figures of yesterday and today, Albert Gallatin never paraded his patriotism, which was sincere and abiding, nor did he ever make a cheap bid for popularity. He simply appealed to reason and intellect.[17]

In the late 18th Century, men in Geneva were better educated and informed than in other European cities, yet they generally did not live above their means.[18] This spirit of frugality and non-frivolous living tempered Albert Gallatin's early years.

When Gallatin and his friend docked in Boston, he was eager to explore this new land. Gallatin traversed from Maine to the western Pennsylvania and from the western frontier to the Mid-Atlantic States. His thick French accent and limited English vocabulary made him seem awkward. The possibility of unprovoked attacks by Native Americans as well as other trials tested him. After his travels, Gallatin decided Virginia held the key to his future prosperity as a land owner.

Albert Gallatin

Thomas Jefferson

In 1783-84, Gallatin built a home, Friendship Hill, on America's western frontier near the border between Pennsylvania and Virginia (now West Virginia). In 1789, at age 27, he became smitten with socialite Sophie Allegre from a wealthy Richmond family. Sophie's mother disapproved of her daughter being carried off to that far-away Pennsylvania frontier. Sophie and Albert's marriage was blissful but short. Five months after they wed, Sophie caught a frontier malady and passed away. Sophie is interned at Friendship Hill. Afterward, a heartbroken Albert contemplated returning to Europe. However, the dangers of the French Revolution persuaded Albert to remain in Pennsylvania. His frontier land-owner dreams morphed into one of local public service and politics.

In 1790, Gallatin was elected into the Pennsylvania State House of Representatives representing Fayette County in the south-western corner of the state. It did not take long for Albert, naturally skilled in finance, to turn into a legislative heavyweight. Gallatin identified with the hard-scrabble Democratic-Republican (i.e., Anti-Federalist) Party. These frontier-minded Democratic-Republicans abhorred the Federalist Party whom they viewed as imposing an overbearing central government.

Gallatin became sympathetic to the insurrectionist during the Whiskey Rebellion. In 1791, the Whiskey Rebellion erupted on the Pennsylvania frontier when President George Washington and his Secretary of the Treasury Alexander Hamilton imposed a federal tax on distilled spirits, including locally distilled whiskey. Naturally, frontiersmen detested this federalist taxation, especially knowing revenues would mostly be spent in the elite East and do little to improve the country's western frontier.

Albert Gallatin thought President Washington and Secretary Hamilton overreacted by crushing the Pennsylvania Whiskey Rebellion. Twenty frontier rebel distillers were arrested, and two were even hanged. In 1801, when the first Democratic-Republican candidate, Thomas Jefferson, became our president, Alexander Hamilton's whiskey tax was repealed.

In 1793, only three years after his election to the Pennsylvania House, Albert Gallatin was elected to the U.S. Senate representing Pennsylvania. He was soon expelled because Federalist Senators successfully asserted Gallatin had not lived in our country the requisite nine years. He was still considered an immigrant, and could no longer serve. That ignominy was followed by falling in love and marrying the second love of his life, Hannah Nicolson. She came from a welcoming and well-connected naval family in Maryland.

By 1794, Gallatin finally had lived in the country the requisite nine years. He was again elected this time to the U.S. House of Representatives representing western Pennsylvania. He was the first influential Congressman from the western side of the Appalachian Mountains. Gallatin opposed many Federalist schemes, such as the Jay Treaty, and the Alien and Sedition Acts – aimed at disadvantaging newcomers to our country. Gallatin's immigrant origins were never forgotten by his opponents. He suffered their insults, and was often derided as that 'foreign Frenchman.' [19]

At the nation's Capital, in Philadelphia, Congressman Gallatin quickly discovered there was little 'financial-public debt' oversight in Congress. Gallatin joined with fellow Democratic-Republican James Madison as the leaders of the newly-formed House Ways and Means Committee. Gallatin believed Treasury Secretary Hamilton's lavish federal spending had placed our nation dangerously in debt. Gallatin believed the government had borrowed too much, spent too freely and paid excessive interest rates. Too easy access to money and credit increased the potential for corruption.[20]

After his time in the U.S. House of Representatives, Albert Gallatin returned to his home on Friendship Hill, Pennsylvania. Gallatin was determined his family should live within its means, just like the government *should be run*. People commented on his frugal attire.

Gallatin liked cigars. His wife Hannah suggested it would be more cost-effective if he'd buy his cigars by the box rather than by the smaller package. When he took her advice and bought a larger lot of cigars, he found his weekly consumption of cigars doubled, thereby not really saving himself any money. He reversed this latest cigar-buying strategy. Gallatin noted, "More was used when it could be dropped from the barrel, while less was used from frequent scarcity." [21] He attempted to apply this home economic principal to aspects of federal finance. He lived what he preached.

Albert Gallatin had a natural gift for mathematics and the patience to study complex financial reports.[22] He humbly stated, "If I have any talent, it is of making a proper use of ascertained facts and of drawing from these legitimate inferences."[23] Gallatin was also self-effacing, level-headed, and an indefatigable researcher.

In 1800, Democratic-Republican Thomas Jefferson was elected over incumbent Federalist President John Adams. Adams' base of support was the elite-minded urban Easterners. Jefferson's base of support was more rural and former immigrant. Jefferson realized his financial understanding was very limited so he chose Gallatin to be his Secretary of the Treasury. Jefferson said, "Albert Gallatin is the only man in the United States who understands …the precise state of the Treasury, and the resources of the country."[24] One of the major goals of President Jefferson, Secretary of State Madison and Secretary of Treasury Gallatin was to reduce or even extinguish the federal debt.[25] Albert Gallatin headed the U.S. Treasury Department for the next 12 years.

Unlike many in the Jefferson Administration, Albert Gallatin felt most akin to the frontiersman.[26] Gallatin was always looking westward. He shared the frontiersman's dislike of taxes, but realized the reduction of public debt was a fundamental issue.

Gallatin believed in scrupulous accounting and in close monitoring of government expenditures. He believed national defense depended on overall economic strength. Gallatin did not believe our country was as militarily vulnerable as Hamilton had concluded and was less eager to spend money on the military. With an ocean separating us from Europe, Gallatin thought the chronic warfare plaguing Europe was much less likely here.

Gallatin felt the government should pay for roads and canals. He believed infrastructure could knit the country together, especially in the under-populated regions, thus encourage future development. This went slightly counter to Jefferson's view, that the already populated states should receive the biggest portion of the federal pie. Gallatin envisioned the first National Road. Much of that idea later became U.S. Route 40, connecting the Ohio Territories with the eastern United

States. To pay for the infrastructure investments, Gallatin believed federal income could be generated by land sales and import duties.

To undermine the Federalist views, President Jefferson once instructed Gallatin to research and expose wrong-doing during the previous Federalist administrations. Accepting Jefferson's challenge, Gallatin came back stating, "Hamilton [and his Federalists] made no blunders, committed no frauds. Hamilton did nothing wrong." Also counter to Jefferson views, Gallatin opposed the institution of slavery. Obviously, Gallatin's influence went far beyond the Treasury Department.

Many viewed the Jefferson Administration as a triumvirate: Jefferson, Madison (Secretary of State), and Gallatin (Secretary of Treasury). Jefferson and Gallatin worked hard to convince Congress to approve the monumental Louisiana Purchase. In 1803, that expenditure squeaked by the House of Representatives by a 59 to 57 vote. During 1804-1806, when Lewis and Clark were making their epic journey, and upon reaching the headwaters of the Missouri River, they named the three forks found there, the Jefferson, the Madison, and the Gallatin Rivers, in honor of the three most influential politicians of the time.

Gallatin reduced the federal debt from over $82 million to less than $76 million during his tenure as Secretary of Treasury despite the $15 million needed for the Louisiana Purchase, a naval build-up to counter the North African Barbary Pirates and the loss of income from repealed excise and salt taxes.

Meanwhile, in Europe, the Napoleonic Wars (1803-15) were pitting France against many European Powers, including Great Britain. Non-belligerent neutral nations, like the young United States, were unwittingly caught-up in this European conflict. American shipping was attacked and American sailors were sometimes forced to fight for warring nations. America chose neutrality to protect its economy from these European ill-winds.

In 1807, the crew from the British Ship *Leopard* boarded the American ship *Chesapeake* and removed four American sailors who the British believed were in cahoots with the French. President Jefferson responded with his ill-conceived Embargo Act. The aim of the Embargo Act was to force Britain and France to respect American merchant shipping during their European War. Thus Britain and France would be deprived of our goods, chiefly cotton and tobacco.

Most historians agree the Embargo Act was an abysmal failure. The Act was a typical example of the law of unintended consequences. This Act hurt the U.S. economy far more than Britain's and it actually benefited the French economy. Cotton and tobacco still ended up in Europe, but now being transported on European ships. American shipping suffered horribly. New England ports were nearly shut down, and the economy headed into a depression. The Act also encouraged smuggling and law-breaking by U.S. citizens. It was a self-inflicted wound on the U.S. economy.[27]

From its inception, Treasury Secretary, Gallatin, believed the Embargo Act a disaster. Gallatin correctly stated, "Governmental prohibitions do always more mischief than had been calculated..." However, the impossible task of enforcing the Embargo Act went to Gallatin's Treasury Department. The Act was rightfully repealed after a dismal 15 months of failures.

Thanks to the unenlightened Embargo Act, between 1807 and 1808, U.S. exports declined by 80 percent and U.S. imports declined by 50 percent. Federal revenues plummeted from $17 million to $7.8 million.[28]

In 1808, James Madison was elected U.S. President. President Madison intended to promote Albert Gallatin to Secretary of State, but Gallatin's prestige was unjustly tarnished because he was the unwilling enforcer of Jefferson's Embargo Act. Years later, John Quincy Adams said that had Gallatin been appointed to Secretary of State in 1809, the War of 1812 might likely have been averted.[29] Instead, Gallatin soldiered-on as Treasury Secretary in the Madison Administration. Without a doubt, Gallatin was the most competent member of Madison's cabinet. Had Presidents Jefferson and Madison heeded Albert Gallatin's advice more often, they would have been more successful presidents.[30]

The year 1809 was rough for the Gallatin's. Albert and Hannah sadly lost their third (of six) child to common infantile sicknesses.

Both Hamilton and Gallatin understood too much government can kill a capitalist economy, but so can too little government, manifested by forces related to rampant greed. Gallatin was against the popular notion that more paper currency in circulation would lead to more prosperity.

In 1791, the First Bank of the United States, a national bank, had been chartered for 20 years by the U.S. Congress. It was championed by the first Treasury Secretary, Alexander Hamilton. Hamilton correctly saw a national bank as a tool to stabilize and improve our nation's credit. Gallatin pushed for renewing that 20-year charter. The bank was deemed successful by many, especially those with a national, versus a regional outlook. Gallatin saw the bank as a safe place to deposit public funds (versus a state bank), and a good way to move funds from one part of the continent to another part. Those hostile to a national bank were well-off businessmen, who preferred state-charted banks that operated with little oversight.

With a pending war with Britain on the horizon (the War of 1812), a national bank would be in a position to lend the country as much as $40 million towards the war effort. A national bank could be the most important single source of wartime loans to our young country. Gallatin's noble idea to re-charter was struck down by Congress. By not re-chartering a national bank, state-charted banks exploded from 88 in 1811, to 246 by 1816. State-chartered banks issued their own currency and were not subject to regulation.[31] The next year, the United States was fighting Britain, and our country found itself in a precarious position funding the War of 1812.

Luckily, three huge banks were able to fund the war. All of these banks were headed by wealthy foreign immigrants. Nevertheless, the cost of the war upset Gallatin's plans to retire the national debt. After the Louisiana Purchase, our national debt was over $80 million. Gallatin was able to bring the debt down to about $45 million just before the war, before it again exploded. Soon after the beginning of the War of 1812, the United States was on the brink of bankruptcy.

President Madison sent Gallatin to Russia as part of a peace delegation. Gallatin was met there by our Russian minister, John Quincy Adams. Peace negotiations moved to Ghent, in present-day Belgium. The three British commissioners were no match for the team of five Americans who included Henry Clay of Kentucky along with Gallatin and John

Quincy Adams. Adams was the nominal chief of the delegation. Nonetheless, Adams was astute enough to realize the real brains behind their peace effort, with any chance of success, lay with Albert Gallatin. Gallatin's calm determination and tactful patience, as well as his broad national view, as opposed to Henry Clay's western viewpoint and Adams' New England viewpoint, were essential. Gallatin handled the meat and potatoes negotiation with the weak financial hand America had to play. The Treaty of Ghent Convention, for good reason, is called Gallatin's Convention.

The War of 1812 ended in a stalemate in 1815. Conditions and boundaries reverted to those at the start of the war. However, there were two stipulations that favored America: 1) Trade would gradually resume between the two countries, proving to be a real boon to our U.S. Treasury, by collecting more import duties; and 2) Britain had to stop supporting Native Americans in North America.

By the time the negotiations were over, Albert Gallatin had been away from his wife and his family for more than 2 years. Gallatin considered finally retiring to Friendship Hill. However, Hannah was less than enthusiastic about returning to that Pennsylvania frontier.

In 1816, as a private citizen, Gallatin was successful in his efforts to charter a Second Bank of the United States, modeled after Alexander Hamilton's First National Bank of the United States. This bank, a private corporation with public duties, was accountable to Congress and the Treasury Department. With pressure from future President Andrew Jackson's administration, this Second National Bank folded in 1836.

In 1816, President Madison offered Gallatin the post of Minister to France. At first, Gallatin was ambivalent, while weighing a lucrative offer to make more money in the private sector. Nevertheless, Gallatin agreed to take his family to Paris and serve as French Minister. After seven mostly delightful years with some small successes and mild frustrations, the Gallatin's returned to the United States. When Gallatin departed France, he was highly respected and admired.[32]

Albert Gallatin returned to America just in time for the convoluted presidential election of 1824. This election, with four candidates, was decided in the U.S. House of Representatives. Gallatin was wary that one of the four presidential candidates, Andrew Jackson, was a reckless militarist. Andrew Jackson did not win in 1824, but he won four years later. After John Quincy Adams was elected, the new president asked Gallatin to be his Minister to Britain. Once again, Gallatin complied. Gallatin enjoyed London much less than Paris. Even so, his thirteen months in London were fruitful, yet arduous and frustrating. He was instrumental in negotiating the border between the U.S. and Britain in the Oregon Territory.

When Gallatin departed London, he said, "He left the British Government in better temper than I found them…and all has been done that was practicable." Before, Albert Gallatin returned to the United States for the last time in 1827, he ended up serving ten years as an invaluable overseas diplomat.

In 1828, the hero of the Battle of New Orleans, Andrew Jackson, was elected President by stoking the fires of sectional differences. Gallatin stated, "I care little about what party and who is in power," although he deemed the popular but uncouth Jackson was unfit to be president. Nevertheless, Gallatin offered to serve in any capacity in the new Jackson administration. However, Jackson swept away nearly all of the previous political professionals, and started en masse the 'Spoils System,' appalling Gallatin.

Gallatin believed in competent and professional civil servants. He realized he was the beneficiary of such a system inherited from the previous Federalist administration. President Andrew Jackson single-handedly dismantled 'professionalism' in the government. His Spoils System was a huge impediment to federal professionalism and was not repaired for more than a half-century, when Chester Arthur became U.S. president.

Before the Second National Bank's charter was about to expire, Gallatin tried to persuade President Jackson to re-charter the Second National Bank. Instead, Jackson turned this issue into a bitter affair, stating national banks stifled state banks, and then he vetoed it. The Second National Bank of the United States went out of existence in 1836.

Hence, from 1836 to 1914, the United States had no central bank. During this 78-year period, there were twelve bank panics, recessions and depressions. No consensus exists on the causes of these economic downturns. But there is little doubt if a well managed central bank had been in existence, as Albert Gallatin had espoused, many of these downturns could have been totally prevented, or at the very least, the major ill effects would have been mitigated.[33]

In 1830, Gallatin and his family moved to New York City. His long-time millionaire friend, John Jacob Astor, who had offered Gallatin business opportunities in the past, invited Gallatin to serve as president of the National Bank of New York. In 1831, Gallatin was elected president of the newly-formed New York University. Gallatin encouraged higher education and said, "It appeared to me impossible to procure our democratic institutions and the right of universal suffrage, unless we raise the standard of general education and the mind of the laboring classes nearer to a level with those born under more favorable circumstances." [34]

Earlier, around 1825, Gallatin first began taking an interest in Native American affairs. While in New York during the 1840's, Gallatin rekindled this interest. He pioneered a series of scholarly works on Native American origins and languages that to this day is considered extraordinary. Gallatin encouraged a friendly assimilation policy toward Native Americans, as opposed to forcing them onto reservations.

As an elder statesman, Albert Gallatin argued against going to war with Mexico and annexing Texas. Prior to the Mexican War, the United States never had acquired territory by violence or conquest. But in 1844, when James Polk, and a protégé of Andrew Jackson, became president, war with Mexico became inevitable. In annexing Texas, Gallatin believed our country had betrayed its purpose, 'to improve the state of the world, to be a model republic.' In his old age Gallatin was having doubts about the evolving character of the country he had adopted and so come to love. To the end Gallatin was a man devoted to peace.[35]

In 1849, Hannah, Albert's beloved wife and companion for 55 years, died. Three months later, at 88 years old, Albert Gallatin, that born-in-Europe treasure who adopted America and gave us his very best unselfish service, passed away. There were no elaborate funeral parades or ceremonies for Albert Gallatin. That is what he wanted. A Philadelphia newspaper stated, "As a diplomatist, no minister from any country, at the great courts to which he was accredited, ever sustained a higher reputation, anywhere, than in the person of Albert Gallatin." [36]

SOURCES:

McCraw, Thomas K, *'The Founders and Finance,'* the Belknap Press of
    Harvard Univ. Press, Cambridge, MA, and London, England, 2012
Walters, Raymond, Jr. *'Albert Gallatin,'* The MacMillan Company,
    New York,NY, 1957

4

Meriwether Lewis (1774-1809)

...One Great Decision Lead to Many More

Meriwether Lewis of the fabled Lewis and Clark Expedition and undoubtedly the darker of the two co-captains, suffered from depression. If living today, he most certainly would have been helped by the latest anti-depressant medications. Sadly, and barely three years after concluding his exceptional leadership in that Corps of Discovery to our Pacific Northwest, Lewis took his own life, aiming one pistol at his head and a second into his chest.

At the tender age of five, Meriwether Lewis lost his father to the American Revolution. His mother remarried. During adolescence, when a boy needs a father most, his stepfather died. A young Meriwether Lewis did his best to be the man of the house to his twice-widowed mother, siblings, and half-brothers and sisters. Even with these hardships, a cousin recalled, Meriwether Lewis displayed amazing perseverance and courage.

In 1791, President George Washington and Secretary of Treasury Alexander Hamilton felt they needed to send soldiers into Western Pennsylvania to suppress those pioneers who refused to pay the new federal tax on 'their-own-distilled' whiskey. Meriwether Lewis served as an Ensign to quell this uprising. Later Ensign Lewis, serving under General 'Mad Anthony' Wayne, was tasked to fight Native Americans in today's Ohio. Serving under Wayne, Lewis was transferred to a company of adept riflemen. William Clark, the much younger brother of George Rogers Clark, was the unit's captain. The four-year older Captain Clark and the lower-ranked, Ensign Lewis soon became great friends.

Meriwether Lewis

William Clark

When Thomas Jefferson was elected our third president, he appointed 26-year old Meriwether Lewis as his Personal Secretary/Aide-de-Camp. Jefferson had well known Lewis's father. They were neighbors from the Charlottesville, Virginia area. Thomas Jefferson, a Renaissance man, became a father-figure to Meriwether Lewis. For about two years, Jefferson personally trained Lewis to the point where Lewis became an amateur scientist. Jefferson was also aware that an often troubled Lewis had bouts of 'depressions of the mind.' It ran in his family.

In 1801, the United States ended at the Mississippi River. On July 4, 1803, far-sighted President Jefferson purchased the Louisiana Territory from France for $15 million, or about 3 cents/acre. This doubled the size of our country. But its cost was twice the federal budget. What did President Jefferson just buy? Jefferson tasked Meriwether Lewis to find out.

Jefferson planned to make Meriwether Lewis the sole Captain of what would-become the Corps of Discovery. That unit was to have one other junior officer. But Lewis wanted his old Army buddy, William Clark, to be made a co-captain. Yesterday, as well as today, a divided military command almost never functions well. Traditionally, the military structure works best with a discreet chain of command. However, President Jefferson astutely relented to Lewis' petition in this matter.

Although Clark became a co-captain, the Secretary of War and Congress did not fully approve of this joint command. Lewis and Clark acted, for the sake of their soldiers, as if they held this joint command during the entire expedition. [37] Without a doubt, this was a brilliant decision on the part of Lewis. At some level, Lewis understood his personal demons and realized he needed Clark.

Lewis and Clark were near opposites. Lewis was a moody, brilliant, high-strung and consummate planner. William Clark, less formally educated, had more practical experience. Clark also had a steadier temperament and was more outgoing and laid back. Clark could better read river routes and had an easy way with enlisted men. Where Lewis was shaky, Clark was strong and vice versa. [38] Both men deeply trusted the other's judgment. And the two of them never disagreed on the many larger-than-life issues they would face over the next two and a half years.

Only about one in a hundred applicants were chosen for the Corps of Discovery mission. In mid-May 1804, nearly four dozen men departed their winter encampment at Wood River, Illinois, crossed the Mississippi River and headed up the mostly unknown Missouri River.

At that time, 1803-1806, co-captains Meriwether Lewis and William Clark melded together the best in their men. The result was an incredibly cohesive Corps of Discovery. Historians have stated something like, 'the Corps of Discovery was greater than the sum of their parts.' Of the four dozen or so men who came under their command, only one man, Sergeant Charles Floyd, died, likely due to acute appendicitis.

Lewis and Clark were not afraid to incorporate Native American ideas and customs. During the winter of 1804-05, at the Mandan Sioux Village north of present day Bismarck, North Dakota, Meriwether Lewis successfully delivered a baby with help from traditional Indian potions, crushed rattlesnake rings. That baby and his mother, Sacagawea, accompanied the Corps for the remainder of their expedition. Over and over again, Sacagawea proved invaluable to the Corps of Discovery. One, of her many contributions, was just being a woman. When potentially hostile Native Americans saw the Corps of Discovery was traveling with a woman and her baby, they correctly figured the Corps was NOT a warring party.

In north-central Montana, when the Corps of Discovery reached a puzzling fork in the Missouri River, Lewis and Clark's gut reaction told them to take the more southern fork. The rest of the 30 or so men believed the route west was along the more western fork of the Missouri River. The men respected their two leader's instincts, and the Corps took the southern fork. Had they taken that western fork, or the Marias River, it would have been the wrong route. Once again, these two brilliant leaders were correct.

President Thomas Jefferson directed Meriwether Lewis keep a journal of the Corps exploits. But there were long lapses in Lewis' journal when no entries were made, likely due to bouts of depression. However, William Clark made entries into his journal about every day. By and large, Lewis was able to keep himself in check. During the worst of times, painfully traversing Idaho's Bitterroot Range during the late summer of 1805, Lewis was especially able to keep his wits about him as he successfully urged his men onward. But on Lewis' 31st birthday, and when he should have been celebrating, he went into another deep depression. He actually felt he hadn't done much with his life! And this was after his men had finally acquired desperately needed horses from the generous Shoshone Native Americans.

After their epic was over, the now famous Governor of Upper Louisiana, Meriwether Lewis was unable to find a woman who would marry him. Clark was more successful and married his Virginia sweetheart, Judith Hancock.

Lewis was also fighting malaria. There is little doubt his body was often ravaged by recurrent bouts of the disease. Contracting malaria was common for those traveling to the West. And it's possible Lewis suffered from more than one of four common strains of malaria, making his condition even more agonizing.[39]

Lewis was also hounded by a demon bureaucratic accountant from Washington D.C.'s War Department who, of course, had never seen the West or the Rocky Mountains. This disagreeable paper-pusher refused to reimburse Lewis for legitimate expenses.[40] It was bad enough that expense records were complicated, hard to maintain and even hard to keep dry. How could an officer account for a buffalo skin bag of Mandan corn purchased from a Native American who could not read or write? What is the procedure for dealing with the value of a branded horse eaten out of desperation? [41] These are examples of the miserable accounting hoops this clerk put Lewis through. Even many of Lewis' more obvious bills were disputed by the War Department. Before long, this bureaucrat claimed Lewis owed the War Department an ungodly sum. No doubt, this fueled Lewis' depression.

In September 1809, hoping to clear-up the financial mess, Meriwether Lewis and an aide set out from St. Louis to Washington D.C. Traveling down the Mississippi River near present-day Memphis, Lewis and his valet diverted from southbound river travel to an overland more eastward route. Intercepting the well-traveled northeastward bound

Natchez Trace Trail route to Nashville, Lewis spent the final night of his life at Grinder's Stand, Tennessee.

Without the outstanding leadership of Meriwether Lewis, the Corps of Discovery would have never been the success it was. And one of Lewis' first leadership moves, recognizing his own limitations, was countering President Jefferson's original plan and asserting William Clark be made a Co-Captain.

William and Judith Clark named their first child Meriwether Lewis Clark.

SOURCES:

Ambrose, Stephen E., *'Undaunted Courage,'* Pocket Books, an imprint of Simon and Schuster UK Ltd. 1996

Burns, Ken, *'Lewis & Clark: The Journey of the Corps of Discovery,'* DVD, Florentine Films, Walpole, NH, 1997

Danisi, Thomas C. and Jackson, John, C., *'Meriwether Lewis,'* Prometheus Books, Amherst, NY, 2009

Jones, Landon, *'The Essential Lewis and Clark,'* Harper Collins Publishers, New York, NY, 2000

5

David Crockett (1786-1836)

...Hardscrabble Frontiersman and Unambiguous Politician

Probably nobody has done more to distort American History than Walt Disney, including Disney's depictions of 'Davey' Crockett. Crockett always signed his name "David." He seldom wore a coonskin hat and was not much larger than of average physique.

David Crockett's grandparents were massacred by marauding Native Americans. However, a half-century later Crockett would 'break-ranks' and stick his neck out for mistreated Native Americans. Throughout his life, political correctness and choosing the path of least resistance were not in Crockett's DNA. Like Daniel Boone, a similar frontiersman born a half-century earlier, David Crockett was a natural rebel and a man always in search of more elbow room.

As a child, David was often being 'rented-out' to help work off his father's debts. Witnessing his father's failures, David strived unsuccessfully to stay out of debt. But he too, tried and failed. On one occasion Crockett, took pains to repay a loan of one silver dollar to the widow of the man who had loaned him the money ten years earlier.

Crockett had little formal education. He could read only with difficulty. Throughout his hardscrabble life, he had many close calls with death. But he philosophized, "If a fellow is born to be hanged, he will never be drowned." [42]

Crockett stated he was unlucky at love. His first love declined him. His second love jilted him. David then concluded, "I was only born for hardship, misery, and disappointment." His third love, Polly, became his wife and bore him two sons and a daughter. After eight years of marriage, a common frontier malady, possibly 'milk sickness,' claimed Polly. Within a few months after Polly's death, practical David wed a widow with two

David Crockett

Sam Houston

children of her own. This relationship with wife, Elizabeth, was sometimes strained due in no small part to David's wanderlust, often hunting for months on end. He remained more often than not financially strapped, but he provided as best as he could by hunting game.

During the War of 1812, David Crockett was inducted as a soldier to fight a rebellious group of Creek Indians. With him were fellow Tennesseans Sam Houston and General Andrew Jackson. While fighting the Creek, Crockett noted those in military authority were often flawed. He viewed Army hierarchy as a caste system. Crockett was most adept at hunting and supplying game for the soldiers, especially during times of famine. Sergeant David Crockett ended his formal military service in March 1815.

During that time, Crockett contracted malaria. Later, when the high malarial fevers hit him for two solid weeks, he nearly succumbed. He almost died in a boating accident on the Mississippi River. Another time he cheated death in an encounter with a bear.

At 40 years old and after an earlier failed bid, Crockett was elected to the U.S. Congress representing western Tennessee. On the campaign trail, Crockett was a colorful character. He often skirted issues and encouraged the crowds to lubricate themselves with whiskey as he spun his yarns, while his more serious opponent stood open-mouthed. His folksy homespun campaigning approach worked. However, once elected to Congress, Crockett seriously championed his constituents, mostly poor farmers and squatters in western Tennessee. His main objective was to make life easier for the common man, like himself, to settle on lands in western Tennessee.

For a short time, David Crockett was a protégée of President Andrew Jackson. Jackson didn't come from the ranks of the eastern aristocracy, as did the six previous U.S. Presidents. However, Jackson was a well-to-do Tennessee planter. David Crockett's background was a far cry from that. Crockett began disagreeing with his mentor Jackson over many issues, with Crockett invariably siding with the underdog, while Jackson sided in the other direction.

The biggest rift between Jackson and Crockett developed over the treatment of peaceful Native Americans living east of the Mississippi

River. Before long Congressman Crockett saw through the duplicity of Jackson's 'Indian Removal Plan.' But Crockett didn't endear himself to his own small farmer constituency by being so pro-Native American either. His opponents, like future president and fellow Tennessean James Polk, blasted Crockett as a traitor to Andrew Jackson and a 'frontier bumkin.' After four years as a Tennessee Congressman, this spokesman and protectorate of the downtrodden and a defender of Native American sensibilities, was defeated in a reelection bid, mostly because of the Jackson forces amassed against him.

Accepting his defeat, Crockett said, "I would rather be beaten and be a man, than be elected and be a little puppy dog." [43] Becoming more disgusted with President Andrew Jackson and his heir-apparent, Martin Van Buren, David Crockett vowed to leave the country and go to the Mexican State of Texas. Crockett stated, "You may all go to hell, and I will go to Texas."

Arriving in Texas at 49 years old, Crockett retained his dream of starting anew. But that was not to be. When Crockett arrived at the besieged Alamo, he was able to make everybody laugh and forget their dire circumstances.[44] But within a couple of months, Crockett and slightly more than 180 other defenders found themselves in the fortified mission, the Alamo in San Antonio de Béxar.

Around 1718, Spanish settlers and missionaries established a mission San Antonio de Valero (named for Saint Anthony of Padua) on the banks of the San Antonio River. The garrison building would be named "the Alamo," meaning "poplar tree" in Spanish. For nearly 100 years that settlement and the old fort, were part of New Spain. By the early 1820's New Spain became its own sovereign nation, Mexico. For about the next ten years, San Antonio and the Alamo were Mexican property.

The locals in this area were a mix of independent-minded Mexicans, living as far as possible from their capital, Mexico City; and a one-time welcomed, but an unruly group of American 'immigrants.' The latter group paid little heed to established Mexican mores, such as the Mexican law banning slavery in its territories. In December 1835, these two groups, and collectively called, 'Texians' defeated and drove Mexican military forces back to the south.

In Mexico City, the ruler of Mexico, Antonio López de Santa Anna, was not going to let this stand. Santa Anna amassed about 1,500 soldiers and marched them north and inland to retake his Mexican Alamo. After a 13-day siege, Santa Anna's soldiers assaulted the Alamo on March 6, 1836. After a heroic, but only two-hour resistance, it was over. All of the Alamo defenders except for a black slave and possibly one woman, perished. Crockett died as he lived, boldly facing opponents with unflinching determination. The Alamo was again Mexican, for a short time.

About six weeks later, David Crockett's friend, Sam Houston, defeated Santa Anna at the Battle of San Jacinito. Soon Texas became an independent republic. However, Mexico did not formally recognize the Republic of Texas and still considered it Mexican territory.

By 1845, nine years after the Alamo, the Republic of Texas agreed to be annexed by the U.S. in order to become the 28th State of the Union and a pro-slavery state. U.S. President James Polk sent troops into Texas and across Texas' Nueces River, the border Mexico considered, and encroached all the way to Mexico's Rio Grande River. The Mexican-American War ensued. U.S. troops didn't stop at the Rio Grande River. They crossed it and went inland as far as Monterrey. U.S. troops also landed at Vera Cruz on the Gulf of Mexico and eventually reached Mexico City. Taking slightly less than two years, the U.S. was victorious. As a result, the U.S. acquired all of present-day Texas, plus California, Nevada, Utah, and large parts of Arizona, New Mexico, and Colorado, and more. Slightly more than a dozen years later, many U.S. junior officers who fought in the Mexican War served prominently, on both sides, during the horrific Civil War.

In early 1861, when Texas seceded from the Union to join the Confederacy, Sam Houston was in angst and against secession. Houston figured Texas, the republic he worked so hard to create, would be in for a real blood-letting in the upcoming War Between the States. He was correct.

SOURCES:
Gronenman III, William, *David Crockett —Hero of the Common Man,'* Tom Doherty Associates LLC, New York, NY, 2005
Wallis, Michael, *David Crocket —The Lion of the West,'* W.W. Norton & Company, New York, NY, 2011

II. WHEN RIGHT AND WRONG WERE BLURRED

6

John Quincy Adams (1767-1848)

...Far-reaching Service with Courage and Integrity

John Quincy Adams might be the only notable link between Presidents George Washington and Abraham Lincoln. Washington appointed the young Adams as minister to the Netherlands. After he had served as the U.S. President, as a fellow legislator, Adams met Lincoln in Congress. Later, Abraham Lincoln was assigned the unenviable role of arranging Adams' funeral.

John Quincy Adams, the son of our second president, was born into a prominent Massachusetts family. For no less than 50 years, John Quincy Adams served our young nation in many capacities. He served as Secretary of State, Congressman, U.S. Senator, Foreign Minister to several European Powers, Peace Negotiator, and not to mention, President of the United States. Although he had little charm or charisma, it is generally thought he had the highest IQ of any U.S. President. Yet throughout much of his career, he remained far from popular. John Quincy Adams was always more concerned with 'doing the right thing' rather than 'playing politics.' This made him many enemies in both political parties and cost him over and over again.

As a young man, he often accompanied his father, John Adams, on diplomatic missions to Europe. John Quincy Adams closely followed and soaked-up issues in France, Netherlands, Russia, Finland, Sweden, Denmark and Poland. He communicated well in a handful of foreign languages, and he could read and write in Latin and Greek. After graduating from Harvard, he preferred a life of academia and law in Boston. Then President George Washington tapped young Adams to be minister to

John Quincy Adams

James Monroe

the Netherlands. His father, John Adams, had to coax his reticent son to accept the position. John Quincy Adams reluctantly adopted the view of his parents, John and Abigail — 'never campaign for public office, and like death, it should not be desired, but neither should it be avoided.'

Serving our young country aboard, Adams worked the diplomatic circles in England, Portugal, Prussia, and later in Russia. After serving as minister to Russia, he was sent to Ghent, in present-day Belgium, to map out the treaty that ended the War of 1812.

During President Thomas Jefferson's first term, John Quincy Adams was elected senator from Massachusetts. Although elected from the political party opposing Jefferson, he found he agreed with Jefferson on such contentious and important issues as the Louisiana Purchase. This incurred him the wrath of his own Federalist Party. That party disowned him. John Quincy Adams often felt friendless during his long political career. He wrote his father, ex-President John Adams, about his loneliness. The elder Adams replied, "You are supported by no party; you have too honest a heart, too independent a mind and too brilliant talents to be trusted by any man who is under the domination of party feelings. ...You ought to know and expect this and by no means regret it. My advice to you is to pursue the course you are in, with moderation and caution, because I think it the path of justice." [45]

When James Monroe became president in 1817, he chose highly effective diplomat, John Quincy Adams, as his Secretary of State. Some historians agree John Quincy Adams was our country's greatest Secretary of State. Among other successes, through negotiations, Adams acquired Florida from Spain. Out west, Adams helped establish the northern boundary between the United States and British Canada along the 49th Parallel. [46] This proved to be the solid long-term turning point for a better relationship between the United States and Britain that has continued to this day.

Adams was also the primary architect of the Monroe Doctrine. The sagacity of the Monroe Doctrine has endured for two centuries. It outlines that lands and peoples in the western hemisphere, or the New World (i.e., North and South America), should be free to develop without undue Old World European influence.

The 1824 U.S. Presidential election, with four major candidates, was hotly contested. Among the four candidates, Andrew Jackson received a majority of popular and electoral votes with John Quincy Adams coming in second. But with Jackson receiving less than fifty percent of the electoral vote, the election was thrown into the U.S. House of Representatives. John Quincy Adams emerged as the U.S. President.

There was already bad blood between Jackson and Adams. They were divergent on many issues. After the 1824 election, Andrew Jackson became particularly embittered towards Adams. Only months after Adams was elected, Jackson and his forces were at work to unseat the new President in four years.

During President James Monroe's 'Era of Good Feeling' tenure, U.S. foreign policy was sailing along well. This was due in large part to Monroe's far-sighted Secretary of State for the past eight years, John Quincy Adams. Aside from successful foreign policy, President John Quincy Adams pushed to modernize the economy. He invested in waterways and canals, improved roads, and upgraded higher education. Adams was often hindered by opposition from Andrew Jackson's supporters. Adams also pushed for the establishment of our National Naval Observatory in Washington D.C.

President John Quincy Adams was sensitive to the predicament of Native Americans during the first third of the 19th Century. Here, Andrew Jackson's supporters especially railed against Adams. John Quincy Adams, a most ethical and scrupulous public servant, was limited to one term as U.S. President when he was defeated by Andrew Jackson. In 1828, Andrew Jackson won all of the southern and western states.

After John Quincy Adams was defeated, he defied the prevailing thought that former presidents should not run for another public office. Adams did. In 1830, Adams was elected as a U.S. Congressman from Massachusetts. As a Congressman, he was able to get reelected for nine terms, or for 17 years, until his death in 1848. He chaired a handful of important Congressional Committees. In Congress, Adams became a leading force for the advancement of science. In 1835, the estate of British Scientist James Smithson was donated to our federal government with the mandate to 'increase and diffuse knowledge among men.' This generous estate was mismanaged and squandered by the federal government. Congressman John Quincy Adams fought hard to get Congress to restore those lost funds and use them for their original purpose as stated by Smithson. Adams' work paid off. Today, our country has nineteen museums, nine research centers and much more that fall under the umbrella of the Smithsonian Institution. The Smithsonian is a wonderful public font for science, history and mostly administered by the federal government.

Besides being morally correct on the treatment toward Native Americans, Congressman John Quincy Adams spoke out against slavery, and called for an end of that institution. His moral stands on slavery and Native American treatment made him many enemies in Congress.

In 1839 off the Cuban Coast, the Spanish Slave Ship, *La Amistad,* was taken over by its prisoners, African slaves. Afterward, the *La Amistad* made its way to the New England Coast. Before long, the United States and Spain were embroiled in an international controversy over the fate of the ship and its cargo of slaves. President Martin Van Buren supported Spain. Congressman John Quincy Adams supported the Africans. By 1841, after a series of appeals, the case of *'La Amistad vs. United States of America'* was brought before the U.S. Supreme Court. Things didn't look well for the Africans. Seventy-three year-old Congressman John Quincy Adams agreed to represent the former African slaves.

Furthermore, five of the nine U.S. Supreme Court Justices were slave-holding Southerners. Nevertheless, Adams challenged the Justices to grant the mutineers freedom on grounds found in our Declaration of Independence. Adams succeeded, and for the first time in our American History, kidnapped Africans won their freedoms in the American Court System. Reportedly, John Quincy Adams never charged for his legal services in his eloquent defense of the Africans aboard *La Amistad.*

In 1848, the 80-year old Congressman, working on legislation, suffered a massive stroke. Two days later and too ill to be removed from the U.S. Capitol building, Adams passed away uttering his last words, "This is the last of earth; I am content." Looking back through the lens of history,

John Quincy Adams contributed much to the well-being of our nation despite the fact his unflinching positions were, at many times, unpopular among his small-minded political contemporaries.

Nearly twenty-seven years before he passed away, Secretary of State John Quincy Adams gave one of his most memorable speeches, on July 4, 1821. This occurred in that fabled House Chamber, where Adams later served for 17 years. It was 45 years after our Declaration of Independence, when Adams said, "...What has America done for the benefit of mankind? ...She [is] the language of equal liberty, of equal justice, and of equal rights ...She respects the independence of other nations while asserting and maintaining her own ...Wherever the standard of freedom and independence has been unfurled, there will her heart, her benedictions and her prayers be ...She is the well-wisher to the freedom and independence of all ...She might become the dictatress of the world, but she would be no longer the ruler of her own spirit..."

SOURCES:
Feinstein Stephen, *John Quincy Adams,'* Enslow Publishers, Inc, Berkeley Heights, NJ, 2002
Jones, Howard, *'Slave Mutiny on the Amistad,'*, American History Magazine, January/February 1998
Kennedy, John Fitzgerald, *'Profiles in Courage,'* Harper Collins Publishers, New York, NY, 1956
Parsons, Lynn Hudson, *John Quincy Adams,'* Rowman & Littlefield Publishers, Lanham, MD, 2001

7

Samuel Worcester (1798-1859)

...Paid a Price for Doing 'The Right Thing'

Samuel Worcester descended from a long line of Christian ministers. In fact, he was a seventh generation minister himself. After graduating from the University of Vermont, Samuel had hoped to go overseas to start his ministerial work. But before he went, he took on more schooling at the new foreign mission school located in Cornwall, Connecticut.

The Cornwall Foreign Mission School's high ideals were primarily to help bring Christianity and western culture to non-white cultures. This would be accomplished by educating foreign students with the hope they would return to serve their own distant native culture as missionaries and educators. Along with a few New England students, most of the school's students came from Hawaii, other Pacific Islands, and Asia, with more than a few Native Americans cultures, including the Cherokee. Soon after its inception, young non-white male students were courting local white gentry females. After only nine years, the school closed down, after confronting this unforeseen reality. Samuel Worcester was a witness to this.

A married Samuel Worcester befriended many foreign students. He developed a special affection for one Cherokee student who took on the name of Elias Boudinot. Boudinot's Cherokee name was 'Buck Watie.' Boudinot changed his name to pay respect to the man who financed his education. After 1826, when Boudinot and other Cherokee were no longer welcomed to get educated in Connecticut, Worcester found his calling. He would go to the Cherokee in the Southeast U.S. And he did.

In north Georgia, the Cherokee welcomed Samuel Worcester. Worcester was given the respectful Cherokee name 'The Messenger.' Besides an educator and a printer, Worcester served as the local postmaster.

Samuel Worcester

Elias Boudinot (Buck Watie)

Sequoyah

As all Native Americans, the Cherokee had a spoken, but no written language. Sequoyah, a crippled old Cherokee, saw that some white men could communicate using 'talking leaves' – being able to read and write utilizing sheets of paper. He knew his people were unable to communicate in this manner. Attempting to free his people from the bonds of illiteracy, Sequoyah worked for 12 years, and was often ridiculed, trying to create a Cherokee Alphabet. Eventually, he was able to distill 86 different Cherokee sounds into symbols. It worked. Sequoyah created an alphabet backward, from the sounds. It took only about one week for a typical Cherokee to learn Sequoyah's new Alphabet. The Cherokee were no longer illiterate! Elias Boudinot and Samuel Worcester utilized Sequoyah's brand-new alphabet to print the Bible, and the first Native American newspaper, the *Cherokee Phoenix*.

George Gilmer, the corrupt governor of Georgia, disliked anybody helping the Cherokee. Gilmer and his Georgia Militia were angling how they could confiscate Cherokee lands in North Georgia and put them into a lottery to make money for themselves and their cronies.

A Georgia law was passed requiring anybody working on Cherokee lands to obtain a 'contrived' Georgia License. The state of Georgia could then arbitrarily deny these licenses to anyone perceived as helping the Cherokee.

Eleven helpful missionaries, including Worcester, did not get these ridiculous Georgia licenses. The state of Georgia threw them all in jail, and sentenced them to four years of hard labor. However, Governor Gilmer was *willing* to pardon the missionaries if they just 'went away.' Nine of the missionaries took the pardons and went away. But Samuel Worcester and one other noble missionary, Dr. Elizur Butler refused the pardons. In 1832, after doing two years of hard jail time in Milledgeville, Georgia, Worcester's and Butler's second Cherokee case was brought before the U.S. Supreme Court.

William Wirt, our nation's longest serving Attorney General, had served in that capacity for twelve years for U.S. Presidents James Monroe and John Quincy Adams. Wirt was a friend to Native Americans. In 1830, the first case Wirt brought before the U.S. Supreme, *'Cherokee Nation versus Georgia,'* Wirt pleaded for the U.S. Supreme Court to void the Georgia laws prescribed on Cherokee lands, stating these laws violated the U.S. Constitution. The Supreme Court would not rule on this particular case. Two years later, a more straight-forward case presented itself to the U.S. Supreme Court. This case *'Worcester versus Georgia,'* involved Samuel Worcester's and Elizur Butler's predicament.

The U.S. Supreme Court ruled favorably for the Cherokee. Wirt, Worcester, Butler, and the Cherokee had finally won in the highest court in the white man's land. Supreme Court Chief Justice John Marshall ruled, "…the citizens of Georgia have no right to enter Cherokee land but with the assent of the Cherokee themselves…"

When U.S. President Andrew Jackson heard the Supreme Court Justice's John Marshall decision, he replied, "Well, Chief Justice Marshal has made his decision, now let him [try to] enforce it!" The President, the Commander in Chief, the Executive Branch of our Government, is the only branch of government with enforcement powers. Even after a favorable U.S. Supreme Court decision, Worcester and Butler remained in prison until the next Georgia governor released them.

Eighteen years before Andrew Jackson's haughty response to the U.S. Supreme Court, during the War of 1812's 'Battle of Horseshoe Bend,' the Cherokee had allied with General Andrew Jackson turning him into a popular hero. Fourteen years later, Jackson's military popularity propelled him to the presidency.

From 1836-1839, our nation's shameful 'Trail of Tears' ensued. The biggest victims of this action were the Five Civilized Tribes – the Choctaw, the Creek, the Chickasaw, the Seminole and the Cherokee.

Realizing all was lost after that disgraceful performance by President Andrew Jackson, a small group of Cherokee, including Elias Boudinot, made plans to relocate to Oklahoma as soon as possible. Elias Boudinot, his well-respected uncle, Major Ridge and his cousin, John Ridge, unsuccessfully tried to persuade all the Cherokee to leave as soon as possible. This Ridge-Boudinot group feared the U.S. government would commit genocide on their people if they remained in the East too long. After all, Governor Gilmer was already putting 'Cherokee lands' into the corrupt Georgia Land Lottery, and making sure his friends got the best parcels from one-time Cherokee land.

Only about 10 percent of the Cherokee heeded the Ridge-Boudinot group's advice: "to leave for Oklahoma soon." The other 90 percent of Cherokee believed such a mass removal would never happen in the 'civilized' America of the 1830's. The Ridge-Boudinot group, along with Samuel Worcester and his family and other more realistic or enlightened Cherokee did leave for Oklahoma within four or five years after Andrew Jackson's arrogant pronouncement. This group of earlier migrants to Oklahoma became known as the 'Old Settlers Group.' They spared themselves much of the terrible travelling woes latter groups would encounter.

However, about 90 percent of the Cherokee remained on their eastern ancestral lands. By 1838, the U.S. Government began forcibly and at gunpoint removing the remaining-in-the-East Cherokee. It was brutal.

During 1838-39, about one fourth of the 16,000 Cherokee enroute to Oklahoma perished. This group and a much larger faction of Cherokee forced to go to Oklahoma came to be known as the 'New Immigrant Group.' The New Immigrant Group (1838-39) blamed the whole 'Trail of Tears' ordeal on the earlier Old Settlers Groups that departed in 1836-37.

In June 1839, three months after the last New Immigrant contingent arrived in Oklahoma, far-sighted Elias Boudinot, his uncle, Major Ridge and his cousin John Ridge, all prominent leaders of the Old Settlers Group, were murdered on the same day, by unknown assassins from the New Immigrant Group. The Cherokee's once promising self government was in tatters. A Cherokee Civil War ensued for the next seven years.

Through it all, missionary Samuel Worcester worked tirelessly to try to reconcile the two Cherokee factions. Twenty years after the last of the Cherokee arrived west of the Mississippi River, Worcester passed away in Park Hill, Oklahoma.

SOURCES:
Ehle, John, *Trail of Tears,'* Anchor Books, a Division of Random House, New York, NY, 1988
Wilkins, Thurman, *'Cherokee Tragedy,'* University of Oklahoma Press, Norman, OK, 1970

John Gorrie

8

John Gorrie (1802-1855)

...Underappreciated Humanitarian Inventor

What would the American South be today without air conditioning? In 1902 Willis Carrier successfully brought air-conditioning to the marketplace, and in the process, became wealthy. But was Carrier really the first American to invent refrigeration? One-half century earlier, the basic principles had already been discovered in Apalachicola, Florida, by Dr. John Gorrie. So it's credible the father of modern air conditioning and refrigeration may not be Willis Carrier but rather Dr. John Gorrie. Besides being a great inventor, Gorrie was also a physician, scientist and a great humanitarian.

There is a question about John Gorrie's father. It is possible John Gorrie was the product of an out-of-wedlock liaison. [47] His mother was likely a Creole from the island of Nevis or perhaps a slave from the Eastern Caribbean. Before long, John and his mother had settled in Charleston, and later near Columbia, South Carolina. In the 1820's, young John Gorrie worked as an apprentice in a local pharmacy. He grounded and mixed herbs and potions and distributed tonics. Deadly fevers wracked the Carolina low country. John, a born idealist, found his life's mission – to enter the medical profession to ease the suffering of those with deadly swamp and lowland fevers.

From 1825-1827, Gorrie went for his medical schooling at Fairfield Medical School in western New York. At that time, Fairfield was one of the best medical schools in the country. John specialized in studying tropical diseases. He learned malaria was more incidental in its occurrence while yellow fever came in waves, killing between 12 and 70 percent of those afflicted.

After five years of practicing medicine in South Carolina, John Gorrie took a 250-mile trip aboard a cotton steamer from Columbus, Georgia, down the Chattahoochee and Apalachicola Rivers to the rowdy cotton port of Apalachicola, Florida. Apalachicola, on the Gulf Coast, is about half-way along Florida's western panhandle. Apalachicola ranked third behind the Gulf Coast ports of New Orleans and Mobile, in terms of seagoing tonnage. Unrefined Apalachicola had plenty of merchants, speculators, transients and brawlers. What the town really needed was a doctor, preferably one familiar with fevers and their treatment. In 1833, John Gorrie became Apalachicola's doctor.

Every summer, from about May to November, much of Apalachicola's population packed up, and head north. 'Real Apalachicolans,' which included Dr. Gorrie, remained behind to brave the unhealthy summers. 'Seasonal Apalachicolans' high-tailed up the rivers to safer climes.[48] Malaria, yellow fever, and other fevers became rampant during the summertime. Malaria means 'bad air' in Spanish. This disease is as old as society itself and has conquered many civilizations. Although the upriver towns were not immune to the fevers, the gulf coastal towns, such as Apalachicola suffered much worse.[49]

Doctor Gorrie was a brave man. He would personally take a small boat out to a diseased-quarantined anchored ship in Apalachicola Bay, where he would find the entire crew either extremely ill or dying. Wearing a mask and gloves, he treated those he could save and disinfected the ship before it docked in town. This safeguard greatly curbed the spread of disease from the ships to the inhabitants of the town.

Besides serving as the doctor, the soft-spoken Dr. Gorrie was soon the postmaster, city council member, bank director, city treasurer, and mayor of Apalachicola. As mayor, he successfully pushed for many needed measures to improve the town's filthy sanitary conditions and practices, including cleaning up the food markets, clearing out trash and weeds, and hopefully draining the nearby swamps.

Gorrie was active in his Episcopal Church. He believed God revealed himself to man via science. He understood everything in nature had a purpose, and that nature's so-called destructiveness was a promise of rebirth.

Doctor Gorrie correctly postulated: 1) there was a link between the fevers and the nearby swamps; 2) fevers were contracted at nighttime; and 3) cooling of the air temperature was incompatible with fevers.[50] He believed cold temperature was a natural healer. Gorrie witnessed a handful of occurrences to support his premise. He noticed when a cold front passed over Apalachicola, it soaked up the moisture-laden air while lowering the air temperature. He also noticed his patients improved with these favorable atmospheric conditions and the changing seasons, summer-to-fall-to-winter, curbed fevers. If buildings up north could be built to keep cold out, why couldn't buildings in the south be built to keep out the heat? [51]

Dr. Gorrie was convinced he had to cool sick rooms to reduce fevers and make his patients more comfortable. How? In the 19th Century, ice was cut from northern lakes during the winters and stored in underground ice-houses. Then this ice was packed in sawdust where it lasted for a long time. Sometimes this ice survived a shipment to the South during the summer, but not always. This was a lucrative business for northern ice-packers, but an unreliable and expensive proposition for Southerners. Gorrie realized it would be less troublesome if Southerners were able to make their own ice. By 1845, Dr. Gorrie gave up his medical practice to focus on ice-making.

Dr. Gorrie knew if air was compressed, it heated up. He postulated if this super-heated air compressed inside metal pipes, could then be cooled down, and then released at room temperature, he might have something. He figured-out how to cool off this hot compressed air inside the pipes with water of ambient temperature. When the once compressed hot air was allowed to decompress, it exited the system cooler, and cold enough to freeze nearby standing water to create ice in pans. His compressor needed to be powered by steam, horse, water, wind-driven sails (and much later by alternating electrical current). The ice collected in the pans would be suspended from the ceiling in a basin placed above a patient's bed. The ice-cooled air, being heavier than warmer air, flowed downward and over the patient with its cooling and comforting properties. This cooler air exited the sickroom through a hole in the floor near the patient.

Dr. Gorrie, showed his new ice machine to some people and explained his findings in scientific journals. One witness to his ice machine was the wager-minded French Consul in Apalachicola. Aware of Gorrie's new invention, the French Consul bragged, "We'd have ice to celebrate with our Bastille Day drinks on July 14, 1850." Many took his wager, because they believed the likelihood of an ice ship arriving from up north was a near impossibility. Naturally, the consul took many bets. Thanks to Dr. John Gorrie's brand new ice machine, he won them all!

In 1851, Dr. Gorrie was granted the first patent for mechanical refrigeration, his new ice machine. He wrote articles for the Smithsonian Institution. But Dr. Gorrie needed to raise venture capital to get his ice machine commercially off the ground and into the marketplace. John Gorrie was not a salesman. Eventually, he found a business partner in New Orleans who required 75 percent interest in his project. However, this gentleman passed away soon after the business agreement was made.

Not only that, fearing a threat to their lucrative business, the lobby of jealous northern ice packers mounted nasty newspaper campaigns smearing Dr. Gorrie. They charged, "Some crank down in Apalachicola Florida, a Doctor John Gorrie, claims he can make ice as good as God Almighty!" [52] This vicious slogan was successful in discouraging other financial backers. Gorrie could withstand insults from ignorant men but he was deeply hurt when so-called learned newspaper men ridiculed him.

Despite the year of his patent, 1851 was a bad year for Dr. John Gorrie. Apalachicola was wrecked by a storm. The boarding house in which he had a financial stake burned down. Dr. Gorrie brooded over his ice machine's failure to reach the marketplace. Even some people in Apalachicola were humiliating him. Dr. Gorrie's health was slipping away.

In 1855, a nearly impoverished Dr. John Gorrie died in Apalachicola. His wife and two children never received any financial recompense for his great invention. [53] Around 1860, his research papers were lost. The concept of air conditioning vanished for 50 years.

By the late 19th century, Congress allowed each state to place two life-size statues of prominent 'state sons' inside National Statuary Hall located in the U.S. Capitol Building in Washington D.C. In 1914, the state of Florida provided a statue of Apalachicola's Dr. John Gorrie, who was finally acknowledged as one of the greatest inventors, and not to mention, a great humanitarian of the 19th century!

SOURCE:

Sherlock, Vivian M, 'The Fever Man, A Biography of Dr. John Gorrie,' Medallion Press, Tallahassee, FL, 1982

Harriet Tubman

9

Harriet Tubman (1822-1913)

...Just Kept Going

Harriet Tubman was an illiterate slave born in Dorchester County on Maryland's eastern shore. Despite her family being split up at slave auctions, Harriet did everything possible to remain close to her parents and siblings. She was a small sickly child, but later as a great Underground Railroad Conductor, she endured feats of remarkable physical stamina.

As a young child, one of Harriet's responsibilities was to rock a white infant to sleep. If the baby awoke and cried, five-year old Harriet was whipped on the neck. Harriet recalled one day she was whipped five times before breakfast. She carried those whipping scars on the back of her neck for the rest of her life. [54]

When she was about twelve years old, inside a dry goods store, Harriet was talking with another slave. This fellow wasn't supposed to be off work. His irate overseer tracked him down in that dry goods store. As this slave was running away, the overseer hurled a two-pound lead weight at the bolting man. The overseer's aim was poor. The lead weight missed its intended victim and struck an undeserving Harriet in the head. The blow knocked her unconscious, and nearly killed her. After Harriet finally came to, she would have migraine headaches for the rest of her life.

In her mid-twenties, and facing the possibility of being sold, Harriet and two of her brothers tried to escape. After several days of wet weather, hunger and confusion, her two brothers decided to turn back. The three returned in defeat to their owner near Cambridge, Maryland. They likely returned to a whipping, but at least they would be dry and fed. Later that same year, and this time by herself, Harriet successfully made it to Pennsylvania Freedom.

About two years later, Harriet made a dangerous trip back to Cambridge, Maryland, to retrieve her husband, John Tubman. John was in less desperate straits because he was a free black man. When Harriet returned to Maryland, John Tubman had found another woman. Although Harriet had risked her life to reach him, he chose to stay with the new woman. Devastated and betrayed, Harriet picked herself up. Not wanting to waste such an arduous and dangerous trip, she soon found a handful of Maryland slaves who were willing to let her lead them to freedom. This was the beginning of her great calling.

In all, it's likely Harriet made thirteen trips and was directly responsible for the successful escape of at least 70 slaves exiting through the swamps of Maryland along the Underground Railroad. Some sources assert she led more than 300 to freedom. Harriet made most of her treacherous trips during the wintertime, knowing potential white pursuers were less inclined to venture out into the winter weather searching for runaways. Also winter nights were longer. This allowed greater distances to be traveled under the cover of darkness. She typically began her getaways on Saturday nights, knowing newspaper notices for runaway slaves wouldn't be appearing until Monday's newspaper. Harriet took pride in the fact she never lost a passenger. Like the biblical hero in the book of Exodus, Harriet was given the moniker, 'Moses.'

Learning from the previous failed escape attempt with her two brothers, years before, Harriet carried a pistol. She carried that pistol as a threat to shoot any of her Underground Railroad passengers, should they get cold feet or week-kneed, thus compromising her mission. She was never known to fire that pistol at anybody. However, she did use the butt end of the pistol to knock out her own painfully infected teeth during one of her escape missions. Before the Civil War, this small broad-shouldered woman was able to get most of her family, including her mother and father, out of the eastern shore of Maryland.

During the Civil War, President Lincoln's January 1863 Emancipation Proclamation reinvigorated Harriet. Later that year, she served as a military scout and spy in the South Carolina Low Country. After some perilous swamp reconnaissance, Harriet was able to guide about 300 Union soldiers through the Combahee River swamps as they raided plantations to help free hundreds of locally enslaved blacks. These new runaways boarded Union steamboats, then headed north for freedom.

By the end of the Civil War, Harriet had served as a nurse and a laundress to many Union soldiers fighting in the South. After the Civil War, with financial assistance from U.S. Secretary of State William Seward, Harriet and her parents settled in Auburn, New York.

After the war, there was correspondence between the illiterate Harriet Tubman and the highly literate Frederick Douglass, two individuals born into slavery. They were born on Maryland's eastern shore and within seven years of each other. In an 1868 letter from Douglass to Tubman, Douglass commented on her many successful nocturnal passages, "The difference between us is very marked. Most that I have done and suffered in the service of our cause has been in public ...I have wrought in the day – you in the night. I have had the applause of the crowd ...while the most that you have done has been witnessed by a few trembling, scarred, and foot-sore bondsmen and women ...The midnight sky and the silent stars have been the witnesses of your devotion to freedom and of your heroism." Tubman and Douglass likely met nearly 20 years earlier when Douglass, living in Rochester, New York, sheltered and hid 13 Canada-bound, Tubman-lead, runaway slaves in his barn.[55]

As an old lady in Auburn New York and always strapped for cash, Tubman maintained a house where indigent black women and wounded black soldiers were taken care of. She used to say, "The Lord told me to take care of my people and that meant for as long as I lived." She also is attributed to have said, "If you are tired, keep going. If you are scared, keep going. If you are hungry, keep going. If you want to taste freedom, keep going." Throughout her long life, Harriet Tubman probably endured more hardships than any other well-known Underground Railroad conductor, yet she outlived all of them.

In 1913, as Harriet was dying, her last words were, "I go to prepare a place for you." In March 1913, Harriet Tubman was buried in Auburn's Fort Hill Cemetery with military honors.

SOURCES:

Bordewich, Fergus, *Bound for Canaan,'* Harper Collins Publisher, New York, NY, 2005

Clinton, Catherine, *Harriet Tubman,'* Back Bay Books/ Little Brown and Company, New York, NY, 2004

Gosman, Gillian, *Harriet Tubman,'* Rosen Publishing Group, New York, NY, 2011

10

Frederick Douglass (1818-1895)

...Fought for Himself; Then Fought for Others

In 1841, Frederick Douglass found his calling. He was asked to give an impromptu speech before a New England meeting of the American Anti-Slavery Society and recount his life as an African-American slave. Douglass was nervous and didn't recall a word he said. But there is little doubt Douglass spoke with passion about his first-hand knowledge on the horrible experiences of being enslaved. Before long, Frederick Douglass was the most influential African American of our nineteenth century, and the conscience of our nation.

Throughout his lifetime, Frederick Douglass spoke and wrote on behalf of many causes such as women's rights and free public education. Douglass was a believer in the equality of all people, whether they be Negro, female, Native American, or recent immigrant. He relished constructive dialogue across racial and ideological divides. Like other Christian-driven abolitionist contemporaries, Frederick Douglass abstained from tobacco and alcohol to keep his body healthy. He could easily spot hypocrisy in clergymen. He abhorred those religious who defended slavery or kept silent about it.

Frederick Douglass believed literacy was necessary for any sustainable freedom for the former Negro slave. He was an early advocate of school desegregation, believing African American children were permanently disadvantaged if they remained in segregated schools. Frederick Douglass also believed Negros should have full citizenship equality and contribute to their community's and their nation's well-being.

Frederick Douglas was born in Talbot County, on the north side of the eastern shore of Maryland's Choptank River, only about 20 miles away from Harriet Tubman's birthplace on the south side of this river.

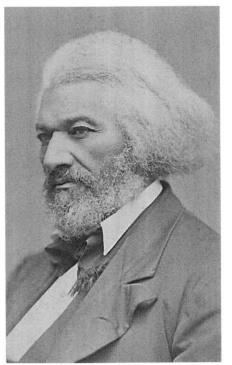

Frederick Douglass

John Brown

Frederick's skin was not as dark as many other slaves. Frederick's father was probably the master of that farm. He barely remembered his mother and never saw her in the daylight. Frederick recalled her lying down next to him as he fell asleep. But before he awoke the next morning, his mother was already gone and working in the fields. Frederick's mother died when he was only six or seven.

Frederick's grandmother took care of the young boy until he was about five years old. As he grew older, Frederick took on tougher work while his frail grandmother was sent into the woods to die, to make more room in the slave quarters.[56] As a young boy Frederick heard of slaves being murdered on the farm for the slightest infractions. He had one searing memory of his aunt being brutally whipped by an overseer.

At about seven years of age Frederick was sent to Baltimore to live with the family of Hugh Auld, a relative of the owner from his eastern shore farm. Sophia Auld, Hugh's wife, began to teach eager Frederick the alphabet and how to read. But upon seeing this, Hugh's response was quick and immediate. Hugh quickly halted Frederick's learning because he knew educating a slave sparked his desire for freedom. When young Frederick was denied a chance to learn, he surmised how important reading and writing were. He figured education was the route from slavery to a sustainable freedom. Frederick also learned there was no slavery in the North.

Young Frederick observed the writings of white men with whom he worked. He asked white children to show him their school books. In time, Frederick was able to secretly teach himself how to read and write. Pretty soon, Frederick was reading newspapers and books. This path of knowledge led Frederick to question, and subsequently to condemn, the institution of slavery. His master, Hugh Auld, began to consider Frederick as troublesome because he correctly suspected Frederick was teaching other slaves how to read and write. [57]

In 1833, Auld had Frederick sent from Baltimore back to Talbot County, Maryland, to work under a particularly cruel overseer. Edward Covey was a sadistic, impoverished farmer with a reputation as a slave-breaker. Covey regularly beat Frederick for the smallest miscues. One time, Frederick collapsed from the field work and Covey kicked him.

Frederick couldn't get up. Then Covey hit Frederick in the head with a wooden slat as Frederick lay in the bloody dirt.

As Covey had hoped, he had just about turned Frederick into a brute, as Douglass himself later acknowledged. Covey had nearly broken Frederick psychologically. Not long after that wooden slat beating, Covey slipped a rope around Frederick's ankles as he prepared to whip him again. Frederick snapped. Forgetting the likely fatal consequences of attacking an overseer, Frederick fought back. The two fought viciously, and eventually Frederick got the better of Covey. This proved a turning point in Frederick's life. After this fight, the embers of freedom that had almost been extinguished by the sadistic Covey, were rekindled.[58] And Covey never again laid a hand on Frederick Douglass.

About six months later, Frederick Douglass was hired out to another nearby plantation where slaves were treated better. Before long, Douglass was teaching as many as 40 neighboring plantation slaves how to read the New Testament. Nevertheless, Douglass' new overseer looked the other way. A slave could receive forty lashes for attempting to learn to read. Nearby plantation owners became incensed and during one of these Sunday gatherings, these white men burst in, clubbing, stoning, and permanently dispersing this black religious congregation.

Later, Frederick Douglass was sent back to master Hugh Auld in Baltimore. He was to work as a hired-out urban slave in the Baltimore shipyards. Douglass became skilled as a ship's caulker, pressing tar and other pliable material into the wooden seams of ship hulls to minimize leakage. Douglass was thus allowed to be employed but he had to return all his earning to his master, Hugh Auld. Eventually, Frederick was able to keep a small portion of his earnings. He used this money to buy books.

Even though Hugh Auld was garnering a healthy portion of Douglass' earnings, frictions between Auld and Douglass escalated. Auld revoked Douglass' hiring-out privileges.[59] Making things even worse, Douglass was soon to be sent back to the plantations on the eastern shore of Maryland. Frederick Douglass resolved to escape while he was still in Baltimore, fearing that if he was sent farther south, it would be that much farther to the border with the free northern states.

In the meantime while in Baltimore, Frederick met Anna Murray, a free black woman. They fell in love. Douglass would have to escape Baltimore with a heavy heart leaving behind his fiancé and friends. With Anna's help, Douglass was disguised as a free black merchant seaman with phony freedman's papers. These papers didn't match Frederick Douglass' description or physique well, except they were of another black man. The ruse worked. The white conductor on the train from Baltimore to Wilmington, Delaware didn't catch it. Douglass then took a steamship from Wilmington to Philadelphia, and another train from Philadelphia to get to New York City.

Arriving in New York City, Douglass felt at least somewhat safe. But he was sleeping on the streets and always worried about slave catchers. Soon Douglass was introduced to prominent black abolitionist David Ruggles. Ruggles accommodated him. His fiancé, Anna, arrived in New York and they were quickly married. Ruggles convinced Douglass and Anna to head for New Bedford, Massachusetts. That city was too far north for most slave catchers, and it had a strong free black community that could protect them. New Bedford also had a whaling industry that welcomed Douglass' skills as a ship's caulker. Frederick and Anna Douglass found the atmosphere in the New Bedford shipyards more accommodating and less racially charged than Baltimore. Life wasn't so bad.

Four months later, Douglass came across a newspaper, *The Liberator*. The newspaper was anti-slavery and published by abolitionist William Lloyd Garrison. It mirrored Douglass' beliefs on the evils of slavery. In 1841, Douglass attended an anti-slavery meeting sponsored by Garrison. When Garrison learned he had a runaway slave in his audience, he asked Douglass to say a few words based on his personal experiences. His story moved many in the audience. Afterward, the American Anti-slavery Society asked Douglass to return and give more speeches.

Before long, Frederick Douglass became an excellent speaker as he related his experiences. He brought large audiences to tears, and moments later had them laughing. Douglass had many powerful sayings on the evils of slavery, including, "No man can put a chain about the ankle of his fellow man without at last finding the other end fastened about his own neck."

Aside from speaking, Douglass also rebutted the pro-slavery propaganda that was flooding the northern press. This propaganda stated how wonderful slavery was for the black man. Douglass countered this propaganda with his own first-hand accounts on the evils of slavery. But all was not easy on the speaking circuit. A pro-slavery mob broke his hand. Some in his audiences couldn't possibly believe such a gifted speaker had actually been born into the ignorance of slavery. [60]

By 1847, Frederick Douglass and Quaker William Lloyd Garrison had a serious disagreement. Garrison believed the institution of slavery made our country so onerous that Garrison wanted to throw out our immoral Constitution. Douglass, upon reading that same document, differed with Garrison. The former slave, Frederick Douglass, believed our Constitution and Declaration of Independence were fine as is, but that Americans ought to live-up to the creed that "all men are created equal."

Douglass believed the Constitution could and should be used as an instrument to fight slavery. Albeit both staunch abolitionists, the divergent views and ill-feelings between Douglass and Garrison never fully healed. However, when Garrison passed away in 1879, Frederick Douglass remarked, at a Washington D.C. memorial service, "It was the glory of this man that he could stand alone with the truth, and calmly await the result."

In 1845, Frederick Douglass published his first book, *The Narrative of the Life of Frederick Douglass, an American Slave.'* The book was a best-seller and moved more northerners to the anti-slavery cause. But by becoming such a public figure, Douglass had made himself more vulnerable. In his book, he didn't share his real name, Frederick Bailey, the manner of his escape, or other details. Nevertheless, Frederick Douglass was in real danger of recapture by slave hunters, and subsequent enslavement in the Deep South. Feeling endangered, Douglass sailed for Britain, leaving his family behind. He arranged for the proceeds of his successful book to go to his wife Anna.

In Britain, Frederick Douglass found hardly any racial prejudice, even significantly less than in the American northern states. In Britain, black folks were treated the same as white folks. No one insulted him! Douglass liked Britain, and thought about sending for his family.

Nevertheless, Frederick Douglass felt compelled to do something for the four million Negro slaves still in bondage in America. He could do very little while in Britain.

Douglass decided to return to the U.S. to see his family and risk recapture. Unexpectedly, two of Douglass' British friends came to his aid. They raised enough money for him to buy his freedom from Maryland's Hugh Auld. Auld received about $700, and signed the papers to legally free Frederick Douglass. After nearly two years in Britain, 28-year old Frederick Douglass returned to America as a free man, with less of a chance of being captured and returned into slavery.

Back at last, Frederick and Anna Douglass settled in the strong abolitionist community of Rochester, New York in 1847. Douglass soon began publishing his own weekly anti-slavery newspaper, *The North Star*. Douglass also started addressing women's rights issues. Douglass believed a Negro's and a woman's lack of civil rights were closely related.

In 1850, our U.S. Congress passed the second heinous Fugitive Slave Act. Runaway slaves were not safe anywhere in the U.S. North. Runaways had to flee farther north into British-controlled Canada. Frederick and Anna Douglass's home in Rochester became a major station on the Underground Railroad for runaways enroute to Canada. Hundreds of men and women passed through the Douglass home.[61] Being involved in the Underground Railroad was risky business, and Douglass could be fined or jailed, under this Second Fugitive Slave Act, for assisting runaways.

Frederick and Anna Douglass raised five children, two daughters and three sons in Rochester. During the 1850's, Frederick Douglass also took-up politics. With tensions heating up between the North and South, white firebrand abolitionist John Brown approached Douglass with a wild idea. John Brown would attack the federal armory at Harpers Ferry, Virginia, steal the armaments and give them to the Negros to free more and more slaves. His growing force would scorch a path southward through the white plantation lands of Virginia and beyond. Douglass told Brown that while it seemed a noble idea, it was bound for failure. Douglass believed John Brown's plan would enrage

Americans and hurt the abolitionist cause.[62] Nevertheless, John Brown proceeded with his outrageous scheme.

John Brown's Raid on the Harpers Ferry armory, in October 1859, was unsuccessful. In the fighting, ten of John Brown's men were killed, including two of his sons. John Brown was captured, tried and hanged. Brown's prophetic last words were, "I am quite certain that the crimes of this guilty land will never be purged away but with blood."

Southerners were shocked when they read accounts of the raid. They began preparing for an impending war with the North. Nevertheless, John Brown became a martyr for the anti-slavery cause. Many insisted Frederick Douglass was complicit. After the John Brown raid, Frederick had to lay low for a good while. But after the Civil War had ended, Frederick Douglass wrote, "Did John Brown fail? John Brown began the war that ended American slavery ...His zeal in the cause of freedom was infinitely superior to mine ...I could live for the slave; John Brown could die for him."

On April 12, 1861, and barely five weeks after Abraham Lincoln was inaugurated our 16th President, Confederate soldiers fired upon the Union garrison at Fort Sumter in Charleston Harbor. The horrible Civil War had begun. Many Southerners and even Unionists believed this war was about states' rights. Yet, early on, Frederick Douglas correctly knew our Civil War would soon be fought over slavery. The first year of the Civil War proved little with small scattered victories on both sides. The subsequent three years were much bloodier. September 17, 1862, was the bloodiest day in American History, when nearly 23,000 soldiers were killed, wounded, or missing at the costly Union victory in Antietam, Maryland.

Politically astute President Lincoln had to wait for the best timing to elevate the Northern cause in the Civil War into the moral issue of abolishing slavery. After that Battle of Antietam, Lincoln found his timing. On January 1, 1863, Lincoln's *Emancipation Proclamation* became official. Slaves in the South were proclaimed free. Our Civil War went to a higher moral plane. It was less of an issue about states' rights and more of an issue about freeing the enslaved Negro. This further infuriated the South. But Frederick Douglass was pleased.

Furthermore, the proclamation kept both Britain and France out of the Civil War. These European powers enjoyed the South's exported cotton, hence they were inclined to support the South. But close to a half-century earlier, Britain and France had already abolished slavery on moral grounds. If Britain and France supported the pro-slavery Southern cause after Lincoln's Proclamation, they would be viewed as big hypocrites.

Frederick Douglass knew knowledgeable blacks would support the cause of the North. Even though Douglass exhorted blacks to volunteer and join the Union cause to end slavery, the North was initially reticent about enlisting Negro soldiers. It took a while, but eventually Negro soldiers were able to get into the fight. Douglass was displeased when he learned black soldiers were paid less than white soldiers, and he worked hard to correct this discrepancy.

In 1863, the African American 54th Massachusetts Infantry was formed. Frederick Douglass championed the unit. Two of Douglass' sons, Lewis and Charles, were among the first to enlist. One year later his youngest son, Frederick Jr., joined his older brothers. In July 1863, the 54th Massachusetts made a heroic but unsuccessful assault on Fort Wagner outside of Charleston Harbor. Close to one-half of its 600 men were lost. The 54th Massachusetts let our nation know African Americans were willing to fight and die for the elevated Union cause to free the Negro slave. Near the end of the Civil War, 200,000 men, or about one-tenth of all Union soldiers and sailors were Negroes. When the Civil War had ended, 38,000 Negro soldiers had given their lives for the Union cause.[63]

Lincoln was assassinated less than one week after Confederate General Robert E. Lee surrendered to Union General Ulysses S. Grant, and barely six weeks after President Lincoln was inaugurated to his second term. Frederick Douglass, like many others, was devastated. Nevertheless, by the end of the Civil War, Douglass was heralded as the leader of Black America.

After the Civil War, in December 1865, the 13th Amendment formally abolished slavery in the United States. After the passage of the 13th Amendment, Frederick Douglass continued on the lecture circuit speaking on behalf of the 14th Amendment, giving citizenship to former slaves. That amendment passed in 1868. In 1870, Douglass successfully lobbied for the 15th Amendment, giving former slaves the right to vote. Douglass, indeed, made enemies in these pursuits. In 1872, his family's home in Rochester was burned. [64]

In 1877, Frederick and Anna Douglass moved to Washington, D.C. and purchased their final home, Cedar Hill. President Rutherford B. Hayes appointed Douglass to the ceremonial post of U.S. Marshall of the District of Columbia. Later President James Garfield appointed Douglass as recorder of deeds for the District of Columbia.[65] In 1882, Frederick's wife of 44 years, Anna, passed away. Within a year and a half, Frederick fell in love and married a much younger white woman, Helen Pitts. Douglass was criticized for his biracial marriage. In response to this criticism, he said his first marriage had been to someone the color of his mother and his second to someone the color of his father.

In 1889, President Benjamin Harrison appointed Frederick Douglass as minister to Haiti. Frederick and Helen Douglass returned to the United States two years later. Douglass continued to speak out for equal rights for Negros and women. In 1895, at age 77, after attending a meeting for woman's rights, Frederick Douglass collapsed and died of likely a massive heart attack. His coffin was transported back to the family plot in Rochester. He was buried next to his first wife Anna. In 1903, his second wife, Helen, joined them both there.

SOURCES:
Becker, Helaine, *Frederick Douglass,*' Blackbirch Press, Woodbridge, CT, 2001
Haffner, Craig, and Lusitana, Dona, *Frederick Douglass, Biography,*' DVD, A&E Television Network, New York, NY, 1994
Squier, Robert, *Who Was Frederick Douglass,*' Grosset & Dunlap, Penguin Group, New York, NY, 2014

III. CIVIL WAR LUMINARIES

11

William Henry Seward (1801-1872)

...*Pragmatic Visionary*

At the start of the 1860 Chicago Republican National Convention, William Henry Seward looked like the most promising candidate to carry the banner of the new Republican Party. In 1856, the Republicans had lost their first presidential bid when Democrat James Buchanan defeated Republican John Fremont. By 1860, Seward had been in Washington for ten years and his manager, Thurlow Weed, was one of the savviest in the country.

Almost everybody at the 1860 Chicago, Illinois convention underestimated Abraham Lincoln. Lincoln was elected, squeaking past Seward, on the third ballot. William Seward noted, "Lincoln had some qualities to make him a good president." [66] Seward also understood during this divisive time, there was much more at stake than his own personal ambition.[67] It did not take long for soon-to-be Secretary of State Seward to become President Lincoln's most trusted subordinate and a devoted, dependable, loyal friend.[68]

President Lincoln astutely realized he needed Seward's superior intellect and wealth of philosophical experience placed high inside his cabinet.[69] Lincoln rarely made an important decision without first consulting his Secretary of State. In effect, Seward became the chief of Lincoln's cabinet and Lincoln made it clear foreign affairs were conducted by Seward's State Department. When Seward took over the department, the atmosphere was politically prickly because of the many Confederate sympathizers in the State Department and elsewhere in the federal bureaucracy. Seward took up the challenge.

William Henry Seward

Abraham Lincoln

Like Lincoln, Seward was not a war hawk. Both men went that extra mile to keep the peace. During the conduct of the Civil War, Seward viewed Lincoln as immensely wise and practical. Lincoln and Seward agreed on merely two demands from the Confederacy, the South re-enter the Union and its institution of slavery be abolished. Both men agreed the South have some say in this matter. During one of their many informal evening chats, President Lincoln said he hoped Seward would succeed him as President and that the Secretary's friends who were so disappointed at the 1860 Republican convention outcome would find things 'made right.' Seward demurred, insisting his political ambitions were now a thing of the past.[70]

William Seward was the fourth of six children of Samuel and Mary Seward. Samuel Seward worked as a farmer, doctor, judge and merchant in New York State. Samuel Seward also had a strong interest in his state's politics and expected his third son, William Henry, to go to college and study law. In 1819, William honored his father's wishes, and afterwards found a teaching job in Georgia. After seeing firsthand the evils of southern slavery, Seward didn't remain in Georgia for long.

Eventually, William joined a law practice in western New York in the town of Auburn. In a chance encounter, after a stagecoach accident in upstate New York, Seward met newspaper publisher Thurlow Weed. Seward and Weed found they were of like mind, believing that government had a major role in improving such infrastructure as roads, canals and schools. The two became lifelong friends. Weed rose to become one of our country's first political bosses and the driving force behind William Seward's future success in politics.

In 1830, Seward was elected state senator from western New York. In 1835, William and his wife Frances visited Virginia. Again, they witnessed how horribly slaves were dealt with. After his trip, Seward's anti-slavery sentiments were further fueled. He viewed blacks as a maltreated race.

In 1839, Seward became Governor of New York. He soon was one of the earlier national politicians to become vocal on the evils of slavery. Seward was perhaps the first politician to coin the well-known phrase, 'Human Rights.' Because of his long-standing and consistent oratory of not wanting slavery to expand, he was even blamed for John Brown's botched raid on Harpers Ferry in 1859. However, Seward had the foresight and the sensitivity to soften his anti-slavery rhetoric as our nation became more divided over this issue. In President Lincoln's cabinet, Seward was often criticized by the 'Radical Republican' constituency for his leniency towards the South.

In 1850, and while serving as U.S. Senator from New York, and hoping to dissuade slavery from taking hold in the Western Territories, William Seward gave his famous anti-slavery 'Higher Law' speech. In it, he stated, "...there is a higher law than the Constitution ...of the common heritage of mankind...bestowed upon by the Creator..." Later, and from the viewpoint of economics, Seward argued, "This nation cannot exist being half slave and half free. It must be one or the other."

Seward accepted two unpopular cases by defending two black men accused of murder. He pleaded for a new legal idea that both of these black men were insane at the time they committed their respective crimes. In both cases Seward was unsuccessful. He also received much hate mail for defending these black men. Friends abandoned him. Nevertheless, during the 1840's, Seward was well ahead of his contemporaries furthering the insanity plea. Starting his service as New York State Senator, Seward pushed for prison reform.

Besides prison reform, Seward believed it was important to make public education available for everyone. He believed education was the best antidote to the poverty of those stuck in the lower echelons of society. Having traveled to Ireland, Seward witnessed firsthand the face of that poverty.[71] Seward often championed 'immigrants' rights.' As New York Governor, Seward went counter to many others, believing in making things less exclusive for immigrants. Seward thought America should be a magnet for immigrants and non-English speaking schools in America were okay. Seward also believed in using federal funds to support needed infrastructure projects such as canals and railroads.

As the Civil War boiled, one wildcard was European intervention. Britain and France were heavily dependent on Confederate cotton. This need favorably colored European support for the South. In 1861, two Confederate diplomats slipped through a Union Naval Blockade near

Charleston, South Carolina. Before long, these two envoys were aboard the British ship *Trent* enroute to England to conduct Southern diplomacy. On open waters, near the Bahamas, and without higher authorization, a Union ship fired a shot across the *Trent's* bow. The *Trent* was boarded and the two Confederate diplomats were forcibly removed from the British ship and taken as Union prisoners.

In the Northern press, the Union captain was hailed a hero, but Britain was so outraged it was ready to go to war with the Union. Seward diffused this situation by arguing for the release of the two Confederate diplomats. Ultimately they were released and boarded another ship bound for Britain. A potential war between the Union and Great Britain was averted. However, after the incident, Seward became unpopular. He had sacrificed himself for the good of the country during an intense situation, going against the grain of the prevailing strong-armed Union naval tactics.

During the Civil War, Seward was often caught up in these most uncomfortable balancing acts. To his right, were the Radical Republicans who only wanted to play implacable hardball with the South. To his left, were those who wished to end the war and let the institution of slavery remain intact. After the war, the Radical Republicans in Congress again lambasted Seward for his conciliatory speech where he stated, "…we are friends again…and we can be nothing else …than be brethren." [72]

In 1862, Seward took aside a French diplomat before the latter was to visit Jefferson Davis and other Confederate leaders. To the southern leaders, Seward relayed this message, "…Tell them, they have no spirit of vengeance from me…they would be cordially welcomed back to their seats in the Senate…I am willing to risk my own political station and reputation in pursuing a conciliatory course toward the South …" After the Civil War, Seward was much in favor of Southern Reconstruction. He stated, "History shows that the more generous and magnanimous the conqueror to the conquered, the sooner victory has been followed by conciliation and a lasting peace."[73]

Just before Lincoln issued the Emancipation Proclamation in 1863, the President believed the best approach for newly-freed blacks was to move them to some place in the Caribbean. Seward disagreed. He correctly realized most freed blacks would not consent to being moved again. Seward's position stated, "I am always for bringing men and states **into** the Union, never for taking any **out**." [74]

In November 1863, just before Lincoln's splendid Gettysburg Address, Seward suggested the country observe a national autumnal day of Thanksgiving. Lincoln saw the wisdom in Seward's suggestion, and formalized Thanksgiving as the holiday we celebrate today.

During the last weeks of the Civil War, Washington D.C. was in a festive mood. William Seward departed his State Department office in a horse-drawn carriage with three other passengers. The carriage driver stopped to fix a malfunctioning door. Suddenly, the driverless team of horses bolted, with them pulling the carriage. The 64-year old Seward tried to work his way to the reins to stop the runaway carriage. Seward fell off, was knocked unconscious, and sustained serious injuries, including a fractured arm and a broken jaw.[75] Seward would be bedridden for weeks.

While John Wilkes Booth was planning the horrific murder of Abraham Lincoln on Good Friday April 14, 1865, he was able to snare a few fellow coconspirators. Lewis Powell, a strapping ex-Confederate soldier from Florida, was willing. While Booth was to assassinate President Lincoln, Lewis Powell was to murder William Seward. Powell muscled his way into Seward's house and bedroom. But his pistol wouldn't fire. Nevertheless, he seriously wounded five in the Seward household including the Secretary of State.

With the butt of his revolver, Powell smashed the head of Seward's son, Fred, exposing his brain in two places. With his large Bowie knife, Powell gashed a guard and two others on the property. Leaving a trail of blood and mayhem, Powell reached the bedridden Seward. Powell repeatedly slashed Seward with the knife in an attempt to kill him. Although Seward was badly cut in the face and neck, a protective jaw splint Seward was wearing as a result of the earlier carriage accident prevented more serious injuries. After three minutes of terror, William Seward and four badly wounded people inside his house survived Powell's vicious attack. Six weeks later, and not fully recovered, William Seward went back to work at the State Department. But sadly, Seward's wife, Frances, was so traumatized by that fateful night she went into an unrecoverable decline and died nine weeks later.

After Lincoln's assassination, William Seward continued as President Andrew Johnson's Secretary of State. Seward, as did others believed our country's future lay in westward expansion. But in Latin American, he espoused a policy of non-intervention. Yet, Seward was intrigued by the possibility of a canal across Central America connecting the Atlantic and Pacific Oceans.[76] In 1866, realizing the navy needed a coaling station somewhere in the Caribbean, Seward tried to purchase the Virgin Islands from Denmark for an agreed $7.5 million. Seward's effort was thwarted by a Congress that labeled him foolish to buy foreign lands. In 1917, when the United States finally purchased the Virgin Islands, the price tag had risen to $25 million.[77]

In 1867, while competing with a potential British offer, Seward negotiated the purchase of Alaska from Russia for $7.2 million. For his farsighted efforts, Seward was parodied in the press: 'The ice crop was the most promising thing;' 'Cattle could sit on ice producing ice cream instead of milk;' and of course, 'Seward's Folly.'

Secretary of State William Seward had a vision for our country. This meant freedom, a unified country and expansion.[78] Seward proved to be a pragmatist. Unfortunately, pragmatists are seldom admired in American politics.

Twelve years after his good friend President Lincoln departed, William Henry Seward succumbed to likely ALS, later to be known as Lou Gehrig's Disease. On his deathbed, he summoned his surviving children. Fully composed, William Henry Seward gently whispered, "Love one another." [79] Like Harriet Tubman, Seward is buried in Auburn, New York's Fort Hill Cemetery. His headstone reads, 'He was faithful.'

SOURCES:
Burgan, Michael, *'William Henry Seward, Senator and Statesman,'*
    Chelsea House Publishers, Langhorne, PA, 2002
Taylor, John M., *'William Henry Seward, Lincoln's Right Hand,'*
    Harper Collins Publishers, New York, NY, 1991

Ulysses S. Grant

Mark Twain

12

Ulysses S. Grant (1822-1885)

...Overachieving Gracious Warrior

One hundred years after the Civil War, and twenty years after D-Day, former General and U.S. President, Dwight D. Eisenhower said, "I think Ulysses S. Grant is vastly underrated as a man and as a general. I know people think this and that about his drinking habits, which I think have been exaggerated ...he took over an army that had a long history of retreating and losing ...he met every test and rose to the occasion unlike I've ever seen in American history. He was a very tough yet very fair man and a great soldier. He's not been given his due ...Grant is very undervalued today. That is a shame because he was one of the greatest American generals, if not the greatest."

Also studying Ulysses Grant's life, this author concurs with Eisenhower's assessment. Yes, Grant often failed at life. He failed at farming and various business endeavors. One could say he failed at everything except for war and marriage. And when Ulysses Grant did succeed in the Civil War, he passed the credit on to others.

Hiram Ulysses Grant was born in 1822 in a small town on the Ohio River upriver from Cincinnati. He was the oldest of six children of Jesse and Hannah Grant. His childhood was unremarkable, but he did have one striking talent. Even as a child, Ulysses Grant showed a gift for handling horses. This was likely indicative of his steadiness and inner calmness.

His penny-pinching father, Jesse, took up business in one of the foulest professions of the day, a tannery. Young Ulysses recoiled and despised the foul smells and bloody sights associated with his father's tannery.

His prospects for a college education appeared dim. However, his father learned about the possibility of a free education for his oldest son at the U.S. Military Academy in West Point. Jesse was able to finagle an appointment for his son. At first, Ulysses refused to go. Nonetheless, in 1839, the strong-armed father was able to send Ulysses on his way to West Point.

Ulysses did like to travel, and the idea West Point was far away appealed to him. In four years, Ulysses finished in the middle of his class. He proved to be especially poor in military bearing and tactics and near the bottom of his class in demerits. He remained a private into his senior year. In spite of this, Cadet Ulysses Grant excelled at mathematics. There was even a possibility he could return to West Point to teach mathematics.

His West Point roommate, Frederick Dent, hailed from outside St. Louis, Missouri. Immediately after West Point, Second Lieutenant Grant was stationed at Jefferson Barracks, near St. Louis and the largest military compound west of the Mississippi River. Frederick Dent had three sisters. Was his good friend Ulysses interested in one of them? The least attractive one, the cross-eyed and the oldest, proved to be the match. Why? Julia Dent was outgoing and vivacious, attributes sorely lacking in his mother, Hannah Grant. Even more importantly, Julia shared his passion for horses. Throughout their married lives, Julia and Ulysses shared one unfulfilled dream, the dream of raising horses. But Julia's father, self-proclaimed 'Colonel' Dent, didn't think young Ulysses showed much promise at anything.

Second Lieutenant Grant's first wartime experience came during the Mexican War. Grant typically was stationed behind the action, serving as a supply and logistics officer, the unit quartermaster. But whenever he heard action, Grant gravitated towards it. In Monterey, Mexicans had his unit pinned down. The Americans were running out of ammunition. When a call went out for someone to run through and return with more ammunition, Lieutenant Grant immediately volunteered. Grant raced his horse, hanging onto the horse's bullet-shielded side through a deadly gauntlet of Mexican gunfire. Grant successfully returned with the horse, carrying the badly needed resupplying ammo.

During the Mexican War, Lieutenant Grant served closely under two of the most prominent generals of the day, Generals Zachary Taylor and Winfield Scott. Grant observed what they did brilliantly, and what they might have done better. Grant appreciated the acumen of General

Winfield Scott, but deemed Scott as pious, a bit high-minded and holding onto obvious political aspirations. Zachary Taylor, on the other hand, dressed plainly, was more down to earth and unlike Scott, didn't care how history would read his decisions. If young Lieutenant Grant were to remain in the army, he would emulate Zachary Taylor rather than Winfield Scott.

Lieutenant Grant hated the horrors of war, the spilled 'blood and guts' associated with battle, yet the drama of it enthralled him. In his memoirs, Grant assessed the U.S. adventure in the Mexican War duplicitously saying, "I believe the Southern Rebellion was an outgrowth of the Mexican War. Like individuals, nations are punished for their transgressions. Our nation was punishment [for the Mexican War] in the most costly war the U.S. would ever see …Our Great Rebellion, fifteen years later."

After the Mexican War, Ulysses married Julia Dent in Missouri. Soon two boys were born. But Ulysses was sent, unaccompanied, to a remote outpost in northern California, under the thumb of a martinet commanding officer. A lonely Lieutenant Grant began drinking. Hence, his reputation as the 'drunken quartermaster' began. Soon, Ulysses resigned from the army to return to his wife and their growing family in Missouri. In one venture after another, farming, merchandizing, real estate, and bill collecting, Grant failed. Earlier, Colonel Dent had given Julia and Ulysses a slave to help with the work on their small farm. Ulysses named the crude house he built on the farm 'Hardscrabble.' Despite his dejection, and when Grant could have sold his slave for a tidy sum, and when he sorely needed cash, Grant gave the man his freedom.

When the Civil War began, Ulysses and Julia had moved up the Mississippi River to work as a clerk for Ulysses' younger brother in the family's leather shop in Galena, Illinois. Seeing the Union threatened with dissolution and many of his friends in the military, Ulysses tried to get re-instated into the Union Army. General George McClellan would not see him because of that reputation as 'the drunken quartermaster.' Finally, Grant received a command of the 21st Illinois Regiment. The previous Colonel of the 21st Illinois was driven into retirement by these rowdy farm boys. It didn't take long for Colonel Grant to develop that love for his men. They responded in kind.

Grant's units waged and won successful small campaigns in Missouri, Kentucky, and Tennessee. In Missouri, Colonel Grant's men were about to attack a like-sized Confederate force. Grant's heart was in his throat as he knew blood was about to be spilled. But when the Confederate Commander, Colonel Harris, heard of Grant's approach, Harris hightailed before Grant attacked. Grant learned an important lesson this day: the unit that first takes the offensive has a big advantage.

In the western theatre, Grant waged small battles in Paducah, Kentucky, Belmont Missouri, and Fort Henry and a bigger assault at Fort Donelson in Tennessee. The first year of the Civil War, 1861, was lackluster for the North. The North had nothing to cheer about until Grant's victories at Fort Henry and again at Fort Donelson in February 1862.

In April 1862, two months after Grant's forces had captured his first Confederate Army at Fort Donelson, Confederate forces surprised Grant's bivouaced forces at Shiloh in southwestern Tennessee. The two-day Battle of Shiloh was the bloodiest battle in our nation's history. More men, on both sides, about 25,000, were lost at Shiloh, than in all previous American wars combined. During the next three years of the Civil War, there would be eight bloodier battles than Shiloh.

Nevertheless, Grant's superior, bureaucratic General Henry Halleck, had to blame somebody for all that bloodshed, even though Shiloh was a Union Victory. Major General Grant was relieved and put on the shelf. Ulysses Grant was miserable.

After about a year of mostly Union failures, President Lincoln overruled General Halleck and insisted General Grant be given another command. Grant was tasked to take the fortress city of Vicksburg, Mississippi. Impregnable Vicksburg is situated on high bluffs overlooking and controlling Mississippi River traffic. President Lincoln regarded Vicksburg as the key to splitting the Confederacy. After some muddling, Grant developed a brilliant plan to take Vicksburg. He would march his men south, on the Louisiana side, across the river from Vicksburg. On two dark nights, Grant's admiral, David D. Porter, attempted to shuttle gunboats and empty troop transport boats past the blazing Confederate artillery fire coming from Vicksburg. Sailing closer to, and hugging, the Vicksburg shoreline, these Union vessels were beneath the range of much of the depressed Confederate artillery pieces. Porter was successful sailing 15 of his 16 vessels, incurring no fatalities, though the Confederate artillery gauntlet past Vicksburg.

About 25 miles below and south of Vicksburg, the transport vessels ferried Grant's troops east across the Mississippi River. After entering Mississippi, Grant's army was cut from its supply lines and had to live off the land. Once in Mississippi, Grant's soldiers marched northeast and fought a few skirmishes before attacking Jackson, Mississippi. After taking Jackson, Grant approached and later lay siege to Vicksburg from its least defensible direction, its eastern backside.

After capturing his second Confederate Army at Vicksburg, Grant was ordered to break the Confederate siege of the Union forces trapped inside the railroad hub city of Chattanooga, Tennessee. A month earlier there had been a Confederate victory at nearby Chickamauga, Georgia. In slightly less than two months, Grant's forces broke the Confederate siege of Chattanooga. President Lincoln knew he finally had found his general in Grant, to end this accursed war.

In March 1864, Grant was summoned to Washington and given command of the entire Union Army. Within 13 months, but with some very costly battles – Wilderness, Spotsylvania Court House, North Anna, Cold Harbor, and the Siege of Petersburg – Lieutenant General Grant ended the Civil War at Appomattox Court House when Confederate General Robert E. Lee accepted peace on April 9, 1865.

Most graciously, General Grant let Confederate General Lee's officers keep their side arms. His own Union Army offered to supply the vanquished Confederates with all the food, clothing and shoes his own army could spare. Just before the formal surrender ceremony, and having empathy for Robert E. Lee, Ulysses Grant said, "What General Lee's feelings were, I do not know? Inwardly glad the war was over? Or sad with the result? My own feelings were sad and depressed. I felt like anything rather than rejoicing at the downfall of a foe who had fought so long and so valiantly, and had suffered so much for a cause …"

After the treaty was signed, Grant's Union Army started hooting and hollering. Grant stepped outside and ordered his Union men to knock it off, saying, "The Confederates are now our countrymen; we will not be rejoicing at their expense." General Robert E. Lee appreciated Grant's magnanimity, and whenever one of Lee's subordinates later badmouthed General Grant, Lee would stop him.

After the Civil War, Ulysses Grant was ambivalent about running for President. But after seeing how horribly Abraham Lincoln's immediate successor, Andrew Johnson, ran the country – and a badly divided country in desperate need of healing – many asked the popular general to run for president. His good friend, General William Tecumseh Sherman, warned Grant saying, "If you go to Washington, they will destroy you." When duty once again called, General Grant responded as he often did. In 1868, Grant was elected our 18th President.

Grant's presidency was mixed. Although, he himself was honest, he had appointed many corrupt politicians to his cabinet. Being basically a poor boy who 'made good,' General Grant was enamored by these cigar-chopping captains of industry. Many were corrupt. If Grant had a weakness, he stayed **loyal** to his friends and to his political appointees longer than he should have. They used him, but he wouldn't use them. Grant used to say, "It's easy to stand by a man when he's right; it's more honorable to do so, when he's wrong."

With his lack of financial experience, Grant had little idea how to handle the financial panic of 1873. He pressed for better treatment of Native Americans. When he was a young soldier in the Pacific Northwest, he became acquainted with Native Americans, and grew sympathetic toward their plight.

When the gains of post Civil War Reconstruction were beginning to be rolled back in the South, Grant stepped in. A handful of times President Grant sent troops into the South to protect the civil rights of African Americans, which were being severely violated. After Ulysses Grant left the Presidency, civil rights for African Americans in the South were stepped-on for the next 80 years. Not until the presidency of Dwight

Eisenhower, would the federal government send the military into the South to protect the civil rights of African Americans.

After his presidency, Ulysses and Julia took a little over two years to sail around the world, until their money ran out. What was supposed to be a private voyage, turned out to be a public goodwill affair, encouraged by President Rutherford Hayes. Wherever Grant went, he was warmly received as the unpretentious face of that late 19th Century American.

Upon their return, Ulysses and Julia settled in New York City where Ulysses worked with their second son, Buck, on Wall Street, for the investment firm, 'Grant and Ward.' Ferdinand Ward was a crook. Ward was building a ponzi scheme, and Buck Grant was unaware of it. Before long, unsuspecting Buck and Ulysses felt the walls tumble down around them. Ulysses sold-off his Civil War memorabilia and the gifts he received from his world tour to pay-off creditors.

Once again, Julia and Ulysses were broke. And it got worse. The persistent pain in Ulysses' throat turned out to be throat cancer. His doctors gave him less than one year to live. Grant accepted the news stoically, but he was wracked with guilt realizing he would leave his beloved wife and four children in a financial bind, after he was gone. He was offered a marginal amount of money to write his memoirs.

Humorist and writer Mark Twain, owned a publishing company, and learned of Grant's predicament. Twain had met Grant years earlier, and in his own memoirs, Mark Twain always spoke highly of unpretentious General Grant. Years earlier, after attending an affair arranged by General William T. Sherman, with General Grant in the seat of honor, Grant was asked to speak. Twain was in the audience. Grant stood up, warmly acknowledged the crowd, and then sat back down. Twain thought this was the most eloquent speech he had ever heard from a public figure – 'just saying nothing.' Afterward, Twain just had to meet Grant. After a meal with Grant, Twain remarked, "It was like having pork and beans with Julius Caesar."

Mark Twain offered Ulysses Grant a much better deal for his memoirs. Although, Grant didn't want to break his word with the first company, Grant's eldest son, Fred, convinced his father to go with Mark Twain's company. Grant was now in a race against death to finish his memoirs. For more than a half-year, through torturing pain, sleepless nights, but pushed by his inflexible iron will, Ulysses Grant plodded on, writing lucidly, poignantly, with generosity to his foes, and loyalty to his friends. Grant produced a considerably longer book than was called for in his contract. But Ulysses Grant always did more than was asked of him …even as he was dying.

Ulysses Grant dedicated his memoirs to 'The American Soldier and Sailor.' He had his final victory, and completed his memoirs just before he died. Even by today's standards Grant's book is considered one of the best written memoirs by any former president. The healthy profits from his 700-page memoirs were more than enough to provide for his wife, Julia, and their four children.

Grant's New York funeral was attended by1.5 million. His pallbearers included two Confederate Generals and two Union Generals. Many have said if the Civil War didn't end at Appomattox Courthouse in 1865, it surely ended twenty years later at General Ulysses Grant's funeral.

SOURCES:

NOTE: For years this author has played, in a one-hour portrayal, Lt. General Ulysses S. Grant. For a six-minute YouTube clip, please visit 'http://www.rickrhodes.com/seminar-topics/general-ulysses-s-grant/'

Bosch, Adriana, and Deanne, Elizabeth *'Ulysses S. Grant, Warrior – President,'* DVD, PBS Home Video –American Experience, WGBH, Boston, MA. 2002

Burns, Ken, *'The Civil War,'* DVDs, Florentine Films, Walpole, NH, and WETA-TV, Washington, D.C., 1990

Flood, Charles Bracelen, *'Grant and Sherman –The Friendship That Won The Civil War,'* Harper Collins, New York, NY, 2005

Flood, Charles Bracelen, *'Grant's Final Victory,'* Da Capo Press, Cambridge, MA 2011

Grant, Ulysses S. *'Personal Memoirs,'* Random House, New York, NY, 1999

13

Joshua Lawrence Chamberlain (1828-1914)

...*Courageous Reconciler*

Union Civil War Brigadier General Joshua Lawrence Chamberlain may have made one of the noblest gestures in human history. This took place three days after Confederate General Robert E. Lee surrendered to Union General Ulysses S. Grant at Appomattox Court House, Virginia. General Ulysses Grant had good reason to select Chamberlain for the honor of accepting the Confederate's formal surrender. Chamberlain participated in more than 20 engagements, and was wounded six times.[80]

The formal ceremony of surrender required Confederate units to stack-up their rifles and battle flags. Chamberlain took it upon himself, going against the grain, and with disapproval from many of his fellow Union Generals, did something quite magnanimous. As the weary Confederate soldiers were stacking-up their rifles, Chamberlain ordered his victorious Union troops, standing at attention behind him, to salute their vanquished Confederate foe!

Joshua Lawrence Chamberlain was the oldest of five children of Sarah and Joshua Chamberlain of Brewer, Maine. He went to school at Maine's Bowdoin College. As a student at Bowdoin, he was part of a group that went out for a noisy intoxicated hayride that upset many of the local town folks. Joshua actually tried to tone down and minimize his friends' intoxicating behavior. But of all who could have been singled out, poor Joshua was the one called on the carpet. He was told to rat on his offending friends or be threatened with expulsion. He refused to rat on his friends.[81] After graduating from Bowdoin College, Joshua married Fanny Adams, and they had two surviving children.

After three years at a theological seminary, Joshua returned to Bowdoin to begin a career as an educator. He became fluent in seven foreign languages.

Joshua Lawrence Chamberlain

John B. Gordon

Chamberlain's theological depth contributed to turning him into an abolitionist. He had asked for a sabbatical from Bowdoin to study in Europe. But instead of going there, Chamberlain answered President Lincoln's 1862 call for more Union volunteers. This 33-year old scholarly married professor was an unlikely candidate to be a soldier. Furthermore, there was talk to appoint him the colonel of the 20th Maine Regiment. Chamberlain declined this offer because he admittedly knew little about soldiering. However, he did accept the second-in-command position. His younger brother, Thomas, also joined the 20th Maine.

In December 1862, the 20th Maine saw action in the Union defeat at Fredericksburg. By June 1863, the colonel of the 20th Maine was promoted. Joshua Lawrence Chamberlain was now in line for the job, and better prepared, to be their next colonel. The great Civil War Battle of Gettysburg was less than a month away.

As the two huge armies were facing-off during the second day at the Battle of Gettysburg, Chamberlain's 20th Maine was tasked to hold the extreme left of the Union line, a piece of high ground known as Little Round Top. It soon became strategically apparent to the attacking Confederates, as well as to the defending 20th Maine, just how important it was to hold Little Round Top. If the Confederates were able to dislodge this thinly-defended Union hill, they could set-up their artillery atop Little Round Top, and rain down havoc from the would-be-exposed left flank of the entire Union Army. The entire outcome of the Battle of Gettysburg was in the balance!

Defending Little Round Top, Chamberlain's 20th Maine withstood repeated Confederate assaults. Running out of ammunition, Chamberlain ordered his men to fix bayonets. Some of the Union defenders charged downhill with their bayonets in a sweeping, hinge-like maneuver into the 15th Alabama's more exposed flank. It worked. Little Round Top was held by the Union. The Union victory at Gettysburg was assured. Later, Colonel Joshua Lawrence Chamberlain received the Congressional Medal of Honor for coordinating his unit's heroics on Little Round Top.

Eleven months later, during the siege of the city of Petersburg, VA, Chamberlain's unit was part of an advance at Rives Salient. The siege of

Petersburg would go on for about nine months. Before the assault Chamberlain would lead, he had a premonition he would die in battle. Leading his men on the battlefield, he grabbed his unit's battle flag from a dying soldier. He was soon shot through both hips and the groin. He refused to fall and braced himself upright with the flag staff and his saber, exhorting his men onward while his boots were filling-up with blood. Blood was soon running out of his pockets. He collapsed and lay on the field for more than an hour before finally getting back to a field hospital. Everyone, including Chamberlain believed his wounds were fatal. Chamberlain was able to pencil 'his last thoughts' to his wife, telling her his mind and heart were at peace, and told her not to grieve too much for him.

But Joshua Lawrence Chamberlain did not die. In a field hospital, next to a badly wounded Confederate Soldier, Chamberlain awoke with the most agonizing of pain. The path of the bullet that severely wounded Chamberlain would not heal well. For the rest of his life the wound was an open conduit for infections of the bladder and testicles. Chamberlain remained in hospitals for about three months. Eventually, he returned to his home in Maine. Six months after his near fatal wound, feeling somewhat better, but against his wife Fanny's wishes, he insisted on returning to his men to serve until the war's end. In another battle, rallying his men, he was again wounded, this time in the chest and arm. Again it was thought Chamberlain would not survive. His arm was almost amputated, but again he rallied.

On April 9, 1865, General Robert E. Lee finally surrendered his haggard Confederate Army to Union General Ulysses S. Grant. It would take about three more days, with a local printing press running day and night to print out all the individual parole papers. These papers granted the former Confederate soldiers unhindered safe passage home.

There was to be a formal ceremony of surrender on April 12, 1865. General Ulysses S. Grant bestowed this ceremonial honor to Brevit Major General Joshua Lawrence Chamberlain and his units. The vanquished Confederate units would march by, stack-up their rifles, and give-up their unit battle flags. Confederate battle flags were stirring symbols of Union resistance.

Chamberlain, always the deep-thinker, understood the gravitas of what was about to take place. He did something extraordinary …and controversial with many fellow Union Generals. As the defeated Confederates approached, Chamberlain ordered his men **to salute the vanquished**, by commanding, 'Order Arms.' 'There was not the sound of trumpet blasts, the roll of a drum, cheers, nor a whisper of vain-glorying. Rather, there was an awed stillness as the Union troops only saluted their vanquished countrymen.'

At the very lead of the Confederate column on horseback, General John B. Gordon of Georgia was heavy-spirited and downcast. But when he caught the significance of this magnanimous gesture by Chamberlain, Gordon returned the salute by bowing his horse's head and dipping his sword. Years later General Gordon recalled his former foe, Joshua Lawrence Chamberlain, was the knightliest soldier he ever knew.

Reflecting on his actions that day, Chamberlain stated, "My main reason, however, was one for which I sought no authority nor asked forgiveness. Before us in proud humiliation stood the embodiment of manhood – men whom neither toils and sufferings, nor the fact of death, nor disaster, nor hopelessness could bend from their resolve; standing before us now, thin, worn, and famished, but erect, and with eyes looking level into ours, waking memories that bound us together as no other bond. Was not such manhood to be welcomed back into a Union so tested and assured?"

This gesture by Chamberlain, and Gordon, lives on in a few wonderful paintings, 'Honor Answering Honor,' and 'Salute to Honor.'

After the Civil War, Chamberlain served four one-year terms as the Governor of Maine. After serving as governor, he returned to his alma mater, Bowdoin College. Chamberlain served on the faculty as a professor and as the president for eight years. But Civil War injuries and discomfort continually plagued him.

From his first election as governor to the end of his life, Chamberlain was active in, and at the forefront, of Civil War Veteran issues and reunions. In July 1888, Chamberlain returned to Gettysburg for the 25th anniversary of that epic battle. To his surprise, he was elected president of the Society of the Army of the Potomac. He continued to make annual pilgrimages to Gettysburg until his death. Joshua Lawrence Chamberlain lived to be 85 years old. His always painful groin wound, inflicted a half-century earlier on the Petersburg battlefield finally got the better of him. It's been said Joshua Lawrence Chamberlain was the last casualty of our Civil War!

SOURCES:
Ashby, Ruth, *'Extraordinary People,'* Smart Apple Media, North Mankato, MN, 1980
Burns, Ken, *'The Civil War,'* DVDs, Florentine Films, Walpole, NH, and WETA-TV, Washington, D.C., 1990
Smith, Diane Monroe, *'Fanny and Joshua,'* Thomas Publications, Gettysburg, PA, 1999

14

Clara Barton (1821-1912)

...A Most Welcomed Pioneer

Clara Barton was born on Christmas Day on a farm in North Oxford, Massachusetts. She was youngest of the five siblings of Captain Stephen and Sarah Barton. Sarah Barton figured she was done having babies at 38 years old. When Clara was born, Sarah's fourth child was already ten years old. By the time Clara was three years old, her older brothers and sister had taught her how to read. Growing up, Clara was a bashful, but energetic tomboy. Not surprisingly, she was also skilled with horses.

When Clara was 11 years old, her brother, David fell from the roof of a barn the family was constructing. David was badly hurt with severe internal injuries. Young, devoted Clara spent two years taking care of him, often at his bedside both the day and night. Clara noticed how fulfilled she felt nursing David back to health.

By the time she was 17 years old Clara had overcome her shyness and became a teacher, the only job available to women outside of the home. On the playgrounds at recess, she played with the bigger boys, thereby gaining their respect. While teaching at another school, an especially unruly boy began taunting her. She called the boy to the front of the class, pulled out a riding whip, and walloped him. Afterward, the boy and Clara were equally shaken, but Clara never had problems with him, nor with anybody else in this class, again. Clara became infuriated when the local school board balked at the idea of not allowing proper schooling for underprivileged mill worker's children, residing in the poorer parts of town. In 1852, when she was 30 years old, she started the first 'free' public school in New Jersey. Soon she had about 600 students. Yet as the school population grew, Clara was not permitted to head it any longer simply because she was a woman. Understandably, Clara soon parted ways with teaching.

Clara Barton

Instead, Clara moved to Washington, D.C. in 1854, and found employment with the U.S. Patent Office. She was quite skilled, but the men working with her often made her life miserable. Ever-changing bureaucratic whims resulted in her pay being reduced. Her outspoken anti-slavery sentiments also hindered her advancement in Washington.

In 1861, the Civil War had begun. At that time, the Union Army had less than 100 male doctors, and most of them were poorly trained. Saws, scalpels, scissors, and liquor were their primary tools. Respectable women were never seen near armies or battlefields.

In 1862, Clara tended to her ill father in Massachusetts. Clara wanted to do something for the Union cause, and her dying father did not discourage her. By the summer of 1862, the Surgeon General handed Clara a written pass permitting her to visit battlefields. Clara soon assembled a small team of nurses. The once shy Clara Barton saw action on sixteen Civil War battlefields, including Cedar Mountain, Second Bull Run, Antietam, Fredericksburg, the Wilderness, and the Siege of Petersburg. She had no qualms treating wounded men from the opposing side of the conflict.

Clara was often in harm's way. Nursing the wounded by candlelight, she sometimes worked on three hours of sleep. One time, a bullet tore through the sleeve of her dress, missing her, but killing the soldier she was tending. Another time, an exploding artillery shell tore away a part of her dress. In 1864, Union General Benjamin Butler placed her in charge of all the 'front line' hospitals in his army. Grateful soldiers called her 'the Angel of the Battlefield.'

As the Civil War was winding down, tens of thousands of letters were arriving at Washington's War Department from families who wished to know the whereabouts, or the fate of their lost sons, brothers, or fathers. President Lincoln, outlined his compassionate vision during his Second Inaugural Address, "...With malice toward none; with charity for all ...let us strive on to finish the work we are in; to bind up the nation's wounds; to care for him who shall have borne the battle, and for his widow, and his orphan." Lincoln later asked Clara Barton to find as many missing soldiers as possible.

Lincoln was soon assassinated, and sadly Clara had little help from the government. Yet she worked on this complex task for four years. Her efforts found 22,000 missing or dead soldiers. Clara also discovered the status of 13,000 Union soldiers who had died at the horrific POW Camp in Andersonville, Georgia. This work left her exhausted. She had a nervous breakdown losing her voice during a speech. But Clara could finally put the Civil War behind her.[82]

In 1869, at the recommendation of her doctor, Clara sailed to Europe, and then traveled to Geneva, Switzerland, where she hoped to restore her health and strength. While there, Clara learned of the International Red Cross. The Red Cross flag is just the reverse of the red field and white cross of the Swiss flag.

Clara also learned about the Geneva Convention. The Geneva Convention was started about 1864 by European combatants. That Convention provided an outline for the relief of wounded and dying soldiers. Clara saw how the Geneva Convention and the Red Cross worked to benefit wounded soldiers on both sides of the battlefields during the Franco-Prussian War (1870-71). Again Clara involved herself in relief efforts for soldiers and other victims of this European war.

In 1873, Clara headed back to the United States intent on making Americans fully understand and appreciate the value of the Geneva Convention and the International Red Cross. She was dismayed and ashamed when her own United States refused to be a signatory to the Geneva Convention, which already had 31 signatories. Clara's health was still far from well. She entered a sanitarium in western New York. In 1877, a healthier Clara resumed her mission to alleviate suffering on the battlefields and elsewhere. She found one of her biggest obstacles was the ignorance of government officials who were suspect of the whole idea of the Geneva Convention. Clara had to make it clear that the Geneva Convention was not a society but a humanitarian treaty, under which relief efforts like the Red Cross could operate.[83] She had to explain that not only during wars, would the Red Cross respond, but also to civilian communities facing natural disasters.

President Rutherford Hayes' administration pooh-poohed her ideas. She waited for the next administration under President James Garfield.

Garfield was much more receptive, and the American Red Cross was on its way in 1881. Garfield's successor, President Chester Arthur, continued to support the Red Cross. In 1882, with Barton's push and Arthur's concurrence, the United States became a signatory to the Geneva Convention. Bold headlines were never made, and there was neither alarm nor joy when the United States signed the Geneva Convention.

In 1884, Clara and her Red Cross were on the scene when the Mississippi and Ohio Rivers flooded. Within a few years, the Red Cross was there for a famine in Texas, an earthquake in California, a tornado in Illinois, and a yellow fever outbreak in Florida. In 1889, the Johnston Flood killed over 2,200. In 1893, a hurricane left 30,000 homeless in South Carolina's Sea Islands. In 1900, the Galveston Hurricane and Flood probably killed 8,000. The American Red Cross was there for all of these catastrophes.

The American Red Cross developed a presence overseas too. In 1896, Clara Barton brought attention and relief to hundreds of thousands of Armenian victims of Ottoman-Turk oppression. In 1898, Barton sailed into Havana Cuba providing supplies to victims of the Spanish-American War. Clara Barton headed the American Red Cross for more than 20 years.

In 1912, on her deathbed, she opened her eyes and spoke, "I saw death as it is on the battlefield; I saw surgeons coming, too much needed by all to give special treatment to any one …I crept around once more, trying to give them at least a drink of water to cool their parched lips, and I heard them at last speak of mothers and wives and sweethearts, but never a murmur of complaint." Upon her death, two days later, one newspaper remarked, "She was perhaps the most perfect incarnation of mercy the modern world has known." [84]

Today, Clara Barton's legacy, the American Red Cross is still a vital organization responding to national and international catastrophes. Clara Barton pioneered the idea humanitarian aid, given for its own sake with no payback in mind, was a most worthwhile endeavor. [85] Other similar organizations have taken their cue from the Red Cross. These include 'Save the Children' (1919, British), 'OXFAM' (1942, British),

'CARE' (1945), 'Doctors Without Borders' (1971, French), 'Habitat for Humanity (1976),' and many others. Clara Barton's handiwork lives on today and hopefully for long into the future.

SOURCE:

Krensky, Stephen, *'Clara Barton Biography,'* DK Publishing, New York, NY, 2011

IV. AMERICAN GROWING PAINS AND BASEBALL

15

Chester Arthur (1829-1886)

...Surpassing All Expectations

Chester Arthur was the 21st President of the United States. In 1881, he was also the fourth vice president to ascend to the presidency upon the death of a sitting president. Along with those three vice presidents before him, Chester Arthur was never elected to the presidency on his own right.

Senator Roscoe Conklin, a three-term senator from New York, was the major Republican political broker of the day. Conklin was the master of political favoritism and corrupt 'machine politics.' Chester Arthur was often viewed as riding Roscoe Conklin's coattails. In 1871 Chester Arthur was appointed as New York City's Commissioner of Customs, thanks to Conklin. In the days before the country had an income tax, the largest source of federal revenues, by far, came from customs duties. Revenues from the Port of New York Customs House accounted for about three-quarters of all these customs duties. The New York City Customs House was the largest federal employer in the entire country, and was notoriously corrupt. Duty collectors were known to accept bribes and skim revenues for themselves. Employees at the New York City Custom House, as well as all other federal agencies, obtained their jobs, for the most part, via the 'Spoils System.'

'To the victor, go the spoils.' This idea was instituted, earlier in the 19th Century during President Andrew Jackson's administration. In other words, there were no professional bureaucrats during most of the 19th Century. Federal positions were handed-out as favors. This federal employment system was inherently corrupt. Chester Arthur knew it.

Chester A. Arthur

James A. Garfield

Like President Ulysses Grant before him, it is generally acknowledged Arthur was not personally corrupt, although he oversaw a corrupt system. Arthur even derided many of his own civil service employees as the 'snivel service.' By best accounts, Arthur remained honorable in a dishonorable profession.[86]

After Abraham Lincoln, the stature of the office of the U.S. Presidency declined. Nonetheless, by the late 1870's, the Republican Party dominated national elections and politics. This proved a recipe for sloth and corruption.[87] However, during this time, the Republican Party was also being strained from within, along the lines of a more than a handful of factions. At Republican Conventions, these factions and their special interests made deal-making and governing a protracted experience.

During the 1880 seven-day Chicago National Republican Convention it took thirty-six ballots to arrive at a presidential candidate. James A. Garfield, a dark horse, finally emerged as the Republican Presidential Candidate. Garfield had risen to Union Major General during the Civil War, and later proved to be a moderate congressman and senator from Ohio. It was politically expedient for Garfield to accept Chester Arthur as his running mate. Arthur, with no previous experience in elected office, was a political operative coming from a large state, New York. Although presidential expectations for the idealist James Garfield were promising, expectations for Chester Arthur were pretty low.

Four months into Garfield's presidency, a deranged office seeker shot him in the back. The wounded president was incapacitated, and there was really nobody holding onto the reigns of the presidency. Two and a half months later, President Garfield succumbed to a wound that was further exacerbated by deplorable medical treatment. Chester Arthur was now the President of the United States. In 1881, when Arthur unexpectedly ascended to the presidency, folks were saying "Chet Arthur? The President of the United States? Good God!"

Watching President Garfield suffer and die, transformed Vice President Arthur. Chester Arthur developed the needed mettle to stand-up to his former mentor, Roscoe Conklin, a great fan of government favoritism. But in doing so, he alienated many Republicans. Chester Arthur had become a maverick in his own political party. In the meantime, and to the chagrin of many Republicans, Ohio Democratic Senator George Pendleton had been trying to clean-up the federal civil service. In January 1883, President Arthur signed the Pendleton Act. That Act started cleaning-up our federal government and setting it onto a path of more professionalism. Using the British system as its model, federal jobs were to be based on qualifications and merit – as most federal jobs are to this day.

Since the end of the Civil War, the U.S. Navy had been in serious decline. Chester Arthur had the foresight to strengthen our weak navy. Obsolete wooden ships were soon replaced with steel ships. This proved fortuitous, because fourteen years later, with a much more capable navy, America's success during the Spanish-American War was assured.

In 1884, Chester Arthur did not win his own Republican party's nomination for a second chance at the U.S. Presidency. When Chester Arthur departed the presidency, he left the office in markedly better shape than it was, three and a half years earlier. He proved to be a friend to good causes and an unyielding opponent to bad measures.[88]

During Arthur's Administration, the President stood up for what he personally believed in: opposing pork barrel legislation, high tariffs, and inhumane immigration laws – aimed primarily at Chinese laborers already in the country.[89] Like John Quincy Adams, more than a half-century earlier, Chester Arthur became a man without a party.[90] Looking at his life in total, Chester Arthur succeeded to be a decent man and a very decent president in an era when decency was in short supply.[91]

SOURCES:
Karabell, Zachary, *'Chester Alan Arthur,'* Henry Holt and Company, New York, NY, 2004
Otfinoski, Steven, *'Chester Arthur,'* Marshall Cavendish Benchmark, Tarrytown, NY, 2010
Rapley, Haberman, Lord, Murphy, Miller, *'Amer. Exp.: Murder of a President,'* DVD; WGBH, Boston, MA, and Corp. for Public Broadcasting, 2016
Time Almanac, *Encyclopedia Britannica*, Chicago, IL, 2008

16

Mary Harris (Mother) Jones (1830? -1930)

... Losing it all, Except her Focus on Others

Mary Harris Jones was born into a poor, and destined to remain poor, family of tenant farmers in County Cork, Ireland. Some sources have Mother Jones being born in 1837, while other sources have her being born in 1830 – making her 100 years old when she passed away. Her father and grandfather rebelled against the injustice imposed by British landlords. Her grandfather was hanged, and her father was about to be hanged, before he made his escape to America. Eight years later, her father had saved enough money to get his wife and three children, including Mary – their oldest daughter, out of Ireland and into North America.

In school, Mary was their sharpest child. She had hoped to become a school teacher. But Mary Jones was disillusioned by the low pay and terrible teaching conditions. So she took up dressmaking. Soon Mary settled in Memphis, Tennessee, where she met her husband, and started a family. Like her father and grandfather, her husband George Jones was outspoken on the awful working and housing conditions of the working class poor. George was active in his Memphis Iron Molders Union. Living in the South during the Civil War, Mary and George Jones also expressed their opposition to slavery.[92]

Within seven years after arriving in Memphis, all four of her young children had died of yellow fever, and George tragically died in an industrial accident. At 37 years old, a devastated Mary Jones was all alone. Her salvation was her ability to look outside of herself, and see the needs of others. Before long, Mary Harris Jones was taking care of other yellow fever victims.

Mary Jones, decided to make use of her sewing skills, and soon moved to Chicago. In her dressmaking work for her well-to-do clients living on Chicago's Lake Shore Drive, she couldn't help but notice the stark

Mother Jones

contrast with others living in poverty in nearby hovels. It burned Mary these upper-crust women cared nothing in the least about the conditions of those less fortunate living right under their noses.

Tragedy struck Mary Jones again. In 1871, four years after moving to Chicago, the Great Chicago Fire destroyed her home, her shop, and all of her worldly possessions. One-sixth of Chicago was destroyed, about 300 were dead, and 100,000 were left homeless. But once again, amidst her great personal pain, Mother Jones was able to look beyond herself. She organized soup kitchens and found shelters for so many left homeless.

One day, in the basement of the homeless shelter where she herself lived, some garment workers were holding a meeting. Mother Jones decided to attend. Their message on the plight of the workers resonated with her to such an extent she spent the next 50 years travelling across America. In doing so, she never had a permanent home. Her heart was too busy promoting the needs of the dispossessed and the many mistreated working poor, especially the children.

Conservatively-dressed and often wearing a bonnet, feisty Mother Jones was no pushover. She spoke the language of the streets, and swore with the best of them to get her messages across. In her time, it was estimated two million children were working in mines, mills, and factories. Destitute children as young as six years old were working 16-hour days in miserable conditions. These children were working out of necessity, and many were maimed with missing fingers and limbs. Mother Jones believed working men ought to be able to earn a decent living wage permitting their wives to stay home and properly raise their children.

Besides exploited children, Mother Jones spoke out on behalf of the textile and railroad workers as well as many others. She especially supported miners. Mother Jones also was a strong advocate of a woman's right to vote in America.

Coal miners often found themselves trapped between a rock and a hard place. In the early 1900's, the death rate of Colorado coal miners was more than twice the national average. Miner pay scales were low and inconsistent. Miners were forced to live in owner-controlled 'company towns,' and paid for their groceries and household goods at the company store, with company script. This company controlled system mimicked the European feudal system of a long bygone era.

Ludlow was one of those company-owned towns in Colorado. The coal miners, organized, pressed for better pay and working conditions, and when that didn't work, they went on strike. They were met by fierce resistance from mine owners. Refusing to give in, the coal miners were evicted from their shantytown shacks. As a result, more than 1,000 striking miners and their families settled in a make-shift tent city near Ludlow.

To make matters worse, the owners of the mine companies hired armed private detective agencies. One of these agencies was Baldwin Felts. The Colorado State Militia was also in the mine company's pocket, carrying out their dirty work. This explosive dynamic came to a head in April, 1914. Probably provoked, Colorado militiamen and Baldwin Felts detectives fired a machine gun and other weapons into the tent city of striking miners and their families. That fateful day of the 'Ludlow Massacre,' twenty were killed, including twelve miners' wives and children. Before it was all over, scores more would lose their lives, with the striking miners taking much heavier fatalities.

After hearing about the massacre, Mother Jones visited Ludlow. Shocked by what she saw and heard, she decided to go to New York and deal directly with the top mine company owner himself, John D. Rockefeller Jr. But the confrontation softened as mother Jones realized Rockefeller had little personal control over the horribly escalating events that April. Over time, he personally regretted the outcome. Many of her long-time supporters were outraged she didn't attack Rockefeller more vehemently. Yet, this might have been the turning point in Rockefeller's personal life, when he shifted from being the unchecked industrialist to the philanthropist he later became.

During her lifetime, Mother Jones was labeled 'the most dangerous woman in America,' and 'the grandmother of all agitators.' She even admitted, "I'm a hell raiser." [93] Her success came by calling attention to the plight of thousands of workers. As a result, federal and state laws were passed, and laws already on the books were finally enforced. In time, besides the United Mine Workers Union, Mother Jones understandably became involved with the Socialist Party of America.

When Mother Jones died in 1930, she wished to be buried in a miner's cemetery next to those coal miners who died in a mine riot 32 years earlier.   On her tombstone, northeast of St. Louis, are the following words: 'She gave her life to the world of labor, her blessed soul to heaven. God's finger touches her, and now she sleeps.'

SOURCE:

Outman, James L. and Elisabeth M., *'Industrial Revolution Biographies,'* Thomson-Gale, Farmington Hills, MI, 2003

George Washington Carver

Booker T. Washington

17

George Washington Carver (1864?- 1943)

...*Educating Himself to Serve Mankind*

During our Civil War, George Washington Carver, his older brother Jim, and their mother Mary were slaves on a modest Missouri farm. The masters of the two young boys and their mother Mary were small-time farmers, Moses and Susan Carver. Moses and Susan treated their slaves much better than many other slave-owners. George and Jim's paternal father, Giles, had worked on a nearby farm, but he died in a farming accident not long after George was born.

When George was a baby, he and his mother were kidnapped by men from Arkansas and held for ransom. Moses Carver went after the kidnappers, and paid their ransom. The kidnappers took the ransom, returned the sick infant, George, but never returned their mother, Mary. Jim and George Carver never saw their mother again. When the Civil War ended in 1865, Jim and George were free to leave, but the childless Moses and Susan Carver, asked the two boys to stay on as part of their family – if they weren't already.

George was a frail and sickly boy, and his family spared him from the harder farm chores. George often worked inside the cabin – cooking, sewing, washing clothes, and tending to the house and garden. This left the inquisitive and highly intelligent George spare time to study nature. 'Aunt' Susan nurtured and tutored George's curiosity about nature. It took little time for young George to surpass his teacher. The study of nature would soon be his life's calling. George learned there was no waste in nature. George developed a special knack understanding what plants needed. He experimented with watering – 'more versus less,' 'sun versus shade,' and other growth variables. In their town of Diamond, Missouri, young George Carver acquired the reputation as 'the plant doctor.'

113

When he was about 12 years old, George said 'good-bye' to Moses and Susan to seek more schooling. George's quest for knowledge led him to public schools throughout Missouri and Kansas. Although many schools did not accept back children, a few did. George earned money and supported himself by cooking, washing clothes and doing other odd jobs. His excellent grades earned him acceptance to a local Kansas College. But when George arrived, college officials saw he was black, and his admittance offer was rescinded.

Deeply hurt, George farmed farther west, while saving his money. About six years after his college rejection, George tried again, this time at a small college in Iowa. George was accepted at Simpson College and was soon appreciated for his intelligence. One of his teachers at Simpson was so impressed with George she suggested he transfer to Iowa State University to study horticulture. Being the first African-American student at Iowa State, he was also one of the best students. He learned to breed two plants together, creating what we know today as a hybrid plant. Before long, George had his Master's Degree in Agriculture and he was teaching classes at Iowa State with solid prospects to remain on their full-time faculty. His reputation growing, George was also receiving offers to teach botany at other universities.

Fifteen year earlier, fellow African American Booker T. Washington started Tuskegee Institute in Alabama. As a former slave, Booker T. Washington was also not afforded childhood schooling. Like Frederick Douglass, Washington understood the importance of education. Washington employed a nonthreatening approach towards educating blacks. His aim was for Tuskegee to become an industrial and agricultural college for rural southern blacks, often victimized by racism. Washington hoped to empower Tuskegee's students with the knowledge they needed for a rewarding life. In the late 1890's, this meant the study of agriculture.

It was impossible for Booker T. Washington to match other monetary offers made to agricultural guru, George Washington Carver. Nevertheless, Carver freely shared with Washington his vision for helping young black students. In 1896, Carver accepted a position as the head of Tuskegee's Agricultural Department. George Washington Carver would never move again.

To say that Carver had a heavy workload at Tuskegee was putting it mildly. He loved teaching, but he had the endless jobs of stocking an empty laboratory, managing two farms, and serving as veterinarian, the chief groundskeeper, and more. As a teacher, Carver inspired his students with his exuberance describing the miracles found in nature, and its sheer beauty.[94]

At Tuskegee, his objective was to make life better for poor southern small-scale black farmers and save them from defaulting on their farms. To this end, George hoped to develop new marketable uses for nontraditional crops. Around the turn of the 20th Century, small-time southern farmers grew almost nothing but cotton. Every year that cotton was planted on the same patch of soil, the soil became less and less productive. Besides severely depleting the soil, cotton crops were subject to ruin by boll weevil infestations. Carver looked for natural ways to enrich the worn-out soil without using expensive fertilizers.

This led Carver to look into 'rotating crops,' season-by-season. George also hypothesized some crops actually replenished the soil. Carver found many legumes, such as peanuts, cowpeas, lentils, and alfalfa enriched the soil by replacing lost nitrogen. Then Carver investigated ways to use these soil-enriching crops to make planting, harvesting, and marketing them a viable financial possibility for poor southern farmers.

George Washington Carver is especially known for his groundbreaking research on the humble peanut. As Carver had hoped, farmers began growing more peanuts, enriching the exhausted soil. Excited by this, Carver set out to find new marketable uses for peanuts. He knew peanuts were loaded with protein and rich vegetable oil. Carver discovered more than 300 uses for the peanut, including about 100 in food recipes, such as flour, paste, milk and cheese. Yet surprisingly, he was not the first one to develop peanut butter. Some of his inedible uses for peanuts include: insulation, face powder, shaving cream, shampoo, paint, soap, medicines, shoe polish, and wood stains.[95]

Carver also found many uses for the sweet potato. He found feeding hogs 'free and plentiful-in-nature' acorns was a suitable replacement for expensive corn meal. George showed farmers how to preserve fruits and vegetables over the winter. His selfless work enriched the lives of countless poor southern sharecroppers. Carver saved the agricultural economy of the rural South. George Washington Carver is considered the father of the science of finding industrial uses for plant products.

George Washington Carver labored not for fame or riches, but rather as a quest for knowledge to help ordinary folks. He turned down a six-figure job offer from Thomas Edison. He never took time to apply for patents, saying, "God gave them to me. How can I sell them to somebody else?"[96] He also believed filing for [so many] patents would take time away from other pursuits, and he would get little else done. Carver believed 'service to mankind' represented real success, rather than the number of patents or the riches derived from such.

George Washington Carver stated, "I am not a finisher ...I am a blazer of trails. Other must take up the various trails of truth, and carry them on." He also said, "Education is the key to unlock the golden door of freedom," and "Nothing is more beautiful than the loveliness of the woods before sunrise."

In 1917, Carver explained his motivation, saying, "Someday, I will have to leave this world. And when that day comes, I want to feel my life has been of some service to my fellow man." In 1943, when Carver passed away after a life of frugality, he was able to donate $60K to his beloved Tuskegee Institute. On his grave, is inscribed, "He could have added fortune to fame, but caring for neither, he found happiness and honor in being helpful to the world."

SOURCES:
Carey, Charles W Jr., *'George Washington Carver,'* Child's World Inc, Chanhassen, MN, 1999
Carter, Andy and Saller, Carol, *'George Washington Carver,'* Carolrhoba Books, Inc, Minneapolis, MN, 2001

18

The Wright Brothers,
Wilbur (1867-1912), Orville (1871-1948)

...Persistence, Grit and Vision

Today, there are well over nine million airplane flights carrying well over 800 million passengers all over the world.[97] Airplanes carry us across continents and oceans in hours, or less. There is no doubt airplanes have knit the world and contributed greatly to global relations and business. Only a century and a quarter ago, this transformation seemed highly improbable.

Two brothers from Dayton, Ohio, Wilbur and Orville Wright, watching heavier-than-air birds fly, believed controlled human flight was likewise possible. Their mother, Susan Wright, had died from tuberculosis when Wilbur and Orville were respectively 22 and 18 years old. The Wright Brother's father, Milton Wright was a well-read United Brethren Church Bishop who encouraged his sons – who never were able to go to college – to read, read, and read. Bishop Milton Wright maintained a huge library in his Dayton home. Beside Wilbur and Orville, Bishop Milton and Susan had two older surviving sons, and a younger daughter, Katherine, and twins who did not survive infancy.

Milton and Susan's two youngest boys, Wilbur and Orville, were especially energetic and often found tinkering. They ate their meals together and kept their money in a joint bank account. They didn't smoke, drink hard liquor or gamble. Even after fame came their way, both men were modest. Nevertheless, they could get into heated arguments.[98] The only Wright sister, Katherine, proved to be a big help to her older brothers, especially as they began finding themselves in the limelight.

Wilbur Wright

Orville Wright

Orville was the more dapper dresser and probably the better mechanic, although Wilbur was no slouch. At academics and sports, Wilbur was more promising, although Orville was no slouch. While playing hockey on a frozen lake, the neighborhood bully took his hockey stick and slammed it into Wilbur's face, injuring him badly. Most of Wilbur's front teeth were knocked out, and he had to be fitted with false teeth.

As a result of this assault, Wilbur developed digestive problems, all the while taking care of his rapidly declining mother. During the next three somewhat reclusive years, Wilbur read more and more of the plentiful books in his father's house. The sadistic boy who had attacked Wilbur with the hockey stick was later convicted of murdering over a dozen people, including his own father, mother and brother. He proved to be one of most notorious murderers in Ohio. He was executed in 1906.[99] How many can say they've been attacked by a mass murderer …and <u>lived</u>?

While Wilbur was recovering from the mouth damage, Orville started a local newspaper, after making a crude printing press. Older brother, Wilbur, found himself interested in Orville's printing business. Wilbur contemplated being a teacher because he felt ill-suited for business. He perceived business as the realm of aggressive, assertive and selfish people, of which he had to exclude himself.[100] Nevertheless, Wilbur was astute enough to realize business affairs made the world 'move.'

In time, both brothers became enamored with bicycling, the same style two-wheeled bicycles in use today. Hence, they opened a bicycle shop. After three years in the bicycle business, Wilbur and Orville were doing reasonably well. More and more people were riding bicycles …and traveling farther and farther from their homes. Successfully riding an upright two-wheeled bicycle required movement, equilibrium and balance. These variables the Wright Brothers well understood and this understanding proved invaluable as their vision of a successful flying machine evolved.

In 1896, it was 25-year old Orville's time for misfortune. Orville had contracted typhoid fever. Their mother Susan had already passed away a half-dozen years earlier. Orville was close to death and remained in bed for six weeks. Older brother Wilbur and younger sister Katherine constantly tended to sick Orville. Wilbur would read aloud many stories and books to Orville. One book especially made an impression on both men. It was about a real-life German glider enthusiast who had recently plunged to his death in a glider accident. Before long, the brothers were reading everything they could get their hands on about birds and how these 'creatures of the air' could glide and fly. The brothers came to believe human flight was indeed possible, despite the overwhelming public opinion of the day, 'God did not intend for man to fly.'

Wilbur wrote to the Smithsonian Institution in Washington for anything and everything it could provide on past experiments with unsuccessful human flight. The Smithsonian Institution complied, and sent the Wright Brothers a wealth of material. The Institution also connected the brothers to the few other folks 'out there' with a similar 'hoping-to-fly' mindset. Non-college educated Wilbur and Orville read and voraciously consumed the plans and notes of those already engaged in aeronautical experiments. They worked on their own, and with no federal subsidization.

Unlike hot air balloons, birds are heavier than air and they can fly with purpose. The brothers were especially transfixed on how big gliding birds, like vultures, near effortlessly stayed aloft, using only their spread-out wings and air currents. Wilbur also noted no bird could soar in a calm.[101]

Wilbur came to the realization it was knowledge and skill that would come from learned experience, rather than brute machinery that would enable man to fly.[102] The brothers believed any heavier-than-air vessel's wings, like a bird's wings, need to be flexible and to warp slightly for that vessel to maintain control and have purposeful flight. Today the Wright Brothers 'wing warping' challenges/technique has been addressed on the rigid wings of modern airplanes with adjustable/controllable elevators, ailerons, spoiler, stabilizers, slats, flaps and rudders and more.

The brothers needed to find a location where they could experiment with their manned flying contraptions – yet to be fully designed. They needed a location with fairly strong and steady winds, hopefully void of trees, and with the potential for not-too-hard landings. Upon inquiring with the U.S. Weather Bureau, Kitty Hawk on North Carolina's Outer Banks seemed to be a sound suggestion.

The Outer Banks, with its steady winds, was also a great place to observe buzzards, gulls, gannets, and large seabirds soar. Outer Banks locals were puzzled by the Wright Brother obsession with watching birds. By the fall of 1900, they were able to get their 'flying machine parts' to Kitty Hawk for assembling. First they flew their glider similar to a kite on a string. To the unsophisticated Outer Bank locals, the Wright Brothers endeared themselves by their solid work ethic, and were known as two of the "workingest boys ever seen." [103]

The brothers built their own camp. They made a stove out of an old carbide can, and geared a bicycle so it could function in the soft sand.[104] Their living quarters on the Outer Banks were Spartan, and they were often assaulted by bed bugs, wood ticks and mosquitoes. During 1901, their second season in the Outer Banks, they were especially tormented by a plague of mosquitoes.

After making many adjustments, their first unpowered manned glider worked. They returned the following year with another and better-refined glider. In 1903, and after three previous seasons using only experimental gliders, the brothers made a fourth trip to Kitty Hawk. December 1903 would be a great success. The Wright Brothers had installed an aluminum engine that rotated 8-foot spruce laminated propellers. The whole contraption weighed 605 pounds.

On December 17, 1903, the brothers made three limitedly successful attempts at powered flights. However, their fourth attempt proved the most successful. Wilbur skimmed 15 feet above the beach for over a tenth of a mile and for a breathtaking 59 seconds. The Wright Brothers had successfully sent a powered machine into the air with a pilot aboard! But many more refinements were needed …and these would come.

As soon as they returned to their home in Dayton, they went to work designing their next airplane. Making future trips back to windy Kitty Hawk, with all of the associated expenses was less necessary. In 1904, they found 84-acre Huffman Prairie. This area was a forty-minute trolley ride northeast of Dayton. The owner let them use the land for free as long as they moved the horses and cows out of the way before their flying experiments.[105] Huffman Prairie turned out to be the site where their flying machines controls were hone and tweaked, and honed and tweaked some more. During 1904, the Wright Brothers had made about 105 flights on Huffman Prairie, honing their machine and especially their own flying skills. They had flown in straight lines, in circles, over 'S-shaped' courses, in calms and in windy conditions. They took flying to a point where it could soon be of great practical use. [106]

Seeing nearly unlimited uses for their new airplane, the Wright Brothers hoped not to take their invention overseas. Thus, they first approached our U.S. government. They wrote to the same federal agency that had already spent $50K on previous failed flight efforts. The U.S. government flat-out rejected the Wright Brothers.

After this, the Wright Brothers welcomed overtures made by British, French, and German interests. It turned out the French interests were the most accommodating. By 1907, Wilbur Wright was in Paris. In1908, one of their flying machines had arrived in Europe badly damaged after transiting the Atlantic aboard a ship. Wilbur had to meticulously repair it. He finally started conducting test flights at a horse racing track near Le Mans, France. Potential French aviators were most favorably impressed, especially by the manner in which Wilbur controlled his flying machine. Wilbur used to say, "The best dividends on the labor invested have invariably come from seeking more knowledge rather than more power." [107] This quote applied to aviation mechanics, but could easily apply to many things.

Wilbur continued making flying demonstration at Le Mans for six months. With his excellent flying skills, it was easy for Wilbur to sell the French on his airplane design. However, it was near equally as important to teach potential French pilots how to handle this new flying machine. Despite being naturally reserved, Wilbur made many friends while in France.

With the overseas news of Wilbur's success in France, the U.S. government finally began to show interest. With Wilbur in France, Orville went to Fort Myer, Virginia, across the Potomac River from Washington, D.C. Orville performed some flight demonstrations with another flying machine. By September 1908, Orville, with his new model, set seven new records at Fort Myer. [108] Then Orville was tasked to take aboard a slightly overweight observer, Lieutenant Selfridge. This was not the first time either brother had flown with a second passenger. President Theodore Roosevelt wanted to 'go up' just days before Selfridge. Nevertheless, this flight on September 17th proved to be a disaster. At about 125 feet high, it appeared a propeller broke apart. Orville tried to glide the disabled craft to the ground, but was less than successful. Upon hitting the ground, Selfridge fractured his skull and was soon dead. Thirty-seven year old Orville was in critical condition with a fractured leg, hip and four broken ribs. Sister Katherine soon was enroute to Washington D.C. to assist hospitalized Orville. The prognosis for Orville to ever fly again was not good.

Until this accident, Wilbur had crashed two times sustaining only slight injuries, and Orville had crashed four times.[109] Years earlier, the two brothers agreed to never 'go up' together in case of a fatal accident. At least one of them would be able to carry on with their shared vision. Once again, Orville survived. Within three months Orville was back in the familiar surroundings of Dayton and well enough to get around on crutches.

By early 1909, Katherine and recovering Orville sailed across the Atlantic to reunite with Wilbur. Wilbur performed more demonstrations, and training for French pilots in Pau, a town near the Pyrenees Mountains in southern France. Along with their technical advances in flight, both brothers, and especially Wilbur, spent much time teaching others how to fly and control their airplanes. In May 1909, Wilbur, Orville, and Katherine arrived back in the United States.

Within two months, with their celebrity status assured, and mostly appreciated by the French, the Wright Brothers were back at Fort Myer for more flight demonstrations. Politicians and dignitaries abounded. A buzz was in the air. But this day, the wind was also blowing at 16 miles per hour. Uncompromising Wilbur, despite all of the pressure by the audience for a 'flight performance,' wisely called off the demonstration with his newest machine. This disappointed many politicians and dignitaries. Despite being let down by the called off flight demonstration, one senator was heard to have respectfully remarked, "I'm dammed if I don't admire their independence. We don't mean anything to them, and there are a whole lot of reasons why we shouldn't."[110] Three days later, with a smaller crowd, their latest flying machine was back in the air, and Orville was at the controls.

For all of the unprecedented glory bestowed on them, Wilbur and Orville Wright had not changed. There was no boasting, no getting too big for their britches.[111] One of Wilbur's last flights was flying together with his brother, Orville, over Huffman Prairie celebrating their many contributions to fixed wing aviation. This was likely the only time these two great pilots ever flew together …after their legacy was assured.

In 1909, the brothers created the Wright Company for the manufacturing of airplanes and incorporated it in New York City. Until the Wright Brothers' successful attempts at heavier-than-air machines, all other attempts were dismal failures.[112] However, as soon as the Wright Brothers succeeded everybody wanted in on the act. In the 1910's advances in aviation were accelerating at a rate few could have predicted.

Since they were children, the brothers hated their picture being taken, primarily because they would have to sit still and 'do nothing' …something unnatural for them. In the more recent past, the brothers often had to shoo away people who were taking close-up pictures of their airplanes, or photographing certain functioning parts or aspects of their flying and controlling mechanics. Regarding flying machines, U.S. patent claims and patent suits were many.

Subsequent patent infringement suits consumed the two brothers. Nine financially-expending lawsuits were brought by them, and three were brought against them. Wilbur and Orville Wright won every one of these decisions.[113] Wilbur was not well suited to wage these many legal battles. These patent fights were physically wearing him down. In early May 1912, Wilbur contracted typhoid fever. By the end of the month and at 45 years old, Wilbur passed away. Orville Wright had hoped to fly as long as he lived. However in 1918 and at age 46, Orville had to give up flying due to the lingering pain caused by his crash at Fort Myer ten years earlier.[114]

Orville did attain a degree of financial success, especially after he sold the Wright Company. But it was far from extravagant. About money, Orville often quoted his father, Bishop Milton Wright, "All the money anyone needs is just enough to prevent one from being a burden to others."

Orville outlived Wilbur by thirty-six years and passed away at 77 years old in 1948. Orville lived to see aviation transformed by jet propulsion, and breaking of the sound barrier,[115] as well as the horrors of World War II.

In 1962, and not even 59 years after Wilbur's and Orville's first powered flights on the Outer Banks of North Carolina, another fellow-Ohioan, astronaut and later-to-be-statesman John Glenn (1921-2016) was the first man to orbit the earth – three times, in his space ship *Friendship 7*. Seven years later, on July 21, 1969, yet another southwest Ohio aviator, astronaut Neil Armstrong (1930-2012), stepped onto the surface of the moon. Aboard Apollo 11's landing craft, *Eagle*, Neil Armstrong made it a point to carry a small swatch of the muslin cloth that Wilbur and Orville Wright used on the wing of their 1903 Flyer! [116]

SOURCES:
McCullough, David, *The Wright Brothers,* Thorndike Press, Farmington Hills, MI, 2015
Tieck, Sarah, *Wright Brothers,* ABDO Publishing, Edina, MN, 2007

Christy Mathewson

19

Christy Mathewson (1880-1925)

...Baseball's Genuine Gentleman

In the days of brawling, hard-drinking, cheating, and rowdy *professional* baseball players, Christy Mathewson, or 'Matty,' went against the grain. Being a devote Baptist, Mathewson, never pitched on Sundays. To many young boys, Christy Mathewson was their hero. And a wholesome star he was. He always had a sense of fair play and he was a tower of character. In February 1936, at the inaugural election to Baseball's Hall Fame in Cooperstown, New York, Christy Mathewson was one of its five first inductees.

Christy Mathewson grew in a small town in northeastern Pennsylvania. At Bucknell University, he starred in baseball, football and served as the class president. From 1900 to 1916, Matthewson was a brilliant Major League Baseball right-handed pitcher. Most of his playing career was spent with the New York Giants. Mathewson had a good variety of pitches, including a brilliant fastball and excellent control. He studied opposing batters, and learned where their weaknesses were. Matty also was a great fielding pitcher.

During his career, he won 373 games, had a .665 winning percentage, and an Earned Run Average (ERA) of 2.13, along with 79 career shutout games. These four statistics, even holding up to this day, place Mathewson at the top echelon of baseball pitchers. In the 1905 World Series, Matty pitched three complete-game shut-outs within a six day period. Many consider this feat the greatest pitching performance in World Series history.

Christy Mathewson would not grant interviews to reporters who he knew had cheated on their wives. But he wasn't a naïve sort either. After his playing days were over, Christy Mathewson was one of the first 'to smell a rat,' when the heavily-favored 1919 Chicago White Sox, later known as the Chicago Black Sox, threw that year's World Series to the lesser-talented Cincinnati Reds. In those days baseball players were underpaid, even on winning teams, like the White Sox. These conditions made it rife for some players to become susceptible to offers coming from unscrupulous gamblers. In the Fall of 1919, gamblers were able to buy-off eight players on the Chicago White Sox. The World Series was thrown. But it didn't take long for the public and the new Commissioner of Baseball to correctly assume there had been a World Series fix. Two years later, the Commissioner banned all eight Chicago White Sox baseball players for life.

In 1918, with World War I going hot and heavy, Mathewson volunteered for the Army's newly-formed Chemical Warfare Corps. His wife, Jane, urged him not to go, but off he went. While serving in France, Captain Mathewson and fellow baseball player, Captain Ty Cobb, were training other soldiers in an active gas chamber. A hand signal was missed. Some soldiers, including Mathewson, were accidentally gassed. With lungs damaged in the gassing incident, Mathewson developed tuberculosis. Within seven years, his weakened lungs contracted pneumonia, and Christy Mathewson died. His last words to his wife were, "Now Jane, I want you to go outside and have yourself a good cry. Don't make it a long one; this can't be helped."

SOURCES:

Burns, Ken and Novick, Lynn, *Baseball,* DVD Florentine Films,
    Walpole, NH, and WETA-TV, Washington, D.C., 1994
Hollihan, Kerrie, *In the Fields and the Trenches:The Famous and the Forgotten
    on the battlefields of World War I,* Chicago Rev. Press, Chicago, IL, 2016
Robinson, Ray, *Matty: An American Hero,* Oxford University Press,
    New York, NY, 1993

20

Lou Gehrig (1903-1941)

...Told Us How Lucky He Was

Lou Gehrig, a native New Yorker, attained his dream of playing for his Major League hometown team, the New York Yankees. In 1923, this humble left-handed first baseman signed with the Yankees. It took Gehrig about two years to become a major force with the Yankees, and when he did, in 1925, he didn't miss a baseball game for the next 14 years! During his career, he set several major league records including grand slams and most consecutive games played. He was a seven-time All Star and a two-time League Most Valuable Player. In 1934, Lou Gehrig was the first Yankee ever to receive baseball's Triple Crown award.[117]

During the 1938 season, Gehrig's playing ability began to slide, and then worsened. He knew something was rapidly falling apart inside his body. On May 2, 1939, after playing in 2,130 consecutive baseball games, Lou Gehrig approached his manager, Joe McCarty, before a game in Detroit. He said for the good of the team he was benching himself, ending a record-setting fourteen-year playing streak. As the announcement came over the loudspeaker, the Detroit Tigers fans gave him a standing ovation. Gehrig sat on the bench with tears in his eyes. He was only 36 years old.

Before Lou Gehrig was born, his mother Christina and father Heinrich had lost two infant daughters and one son. Lou's parents, especially his mother, were compelled to take special care of their only child. Lou formed a strong bond with his mother that would last his lifetime. Lou did grow up to be solid and strong.

Lou grew up in a German working class section of New York, Yorkville. Lou's parents and even young Lou took on various menial jobs to make ends meet. During World War I, prejudice against Germans living in New York City was commonplace, and the Gehrig family felt it.

Lou Gehrig

'Babe' Ruth

In high school Lou worked hard at sports. He played soccer, football and baseball. Oddly, baseball was his weakest sport. In football, he was a bone-rattling tackler, and it was hard for others to tackle him because of his strong legs. His Commerce High School baseball team was invited to play Chicago's best team in Wrigley Field. His protective mother almost didn't allow Lou to make the train ride to Chicago. During the championship game, Lou didn't do much until his last at bat. Late in the game, with the bases loaded and two outs Lou cranked a grand slam insuring New York's Commerce High School victory over Chicago's best high school.

After high school, Lou remained in New York so he could play both baseball and football at Columbia University. Some of his peers at Columbia felt he wasn't good enough to be a student at Columbia.[118]

In 1923, the New York Yankees signed Lou Gehrig for an amount that was modest even by the day's standards, but it was enough to pull Lou and his family out of poverty. In his early years, Gehrig's was a heavy-footed first baseman and unsure where to throw next. In those days, veteran players harassed rookies. His teammates gave him a few nicknames, including 'Tanglefoot.' Gehrig once found some veterans had sawed his favorite bat into four pieces.[119]

By his third spring training, Gehrig proved himself with ability and power. Yankee Manager Miller Huggins especially appreciated Gehrig's character and maturity. Gehrig was soft-spoken; but when he did speak, he was sincere. On June 2, 1925, Lou Gehrig pinched-hit for the Yankee's solid veteran first baseman, Wally Pipp. Earlier, Pipp was struck in the head by a ground ball and taken out of the game. When Pipp was replaced, Gehrig began a phenomenal feat that was not broken until Baltimore Oriole's Cal Ripken's broke it more than a half-century later.

By 1925, homerun slugger Babe Ruth and Lou Gehrig's were the Yankee's one-two punch, with Ruth batting third and Gehrig batting fourth. 'Murderer's Row' was the nickname given the first six fearsome hitters of the late 1920's Yankee line-up, including Gehrig and Ruth. But more-often-than-not Gehrig was in the shadow of Babe Ruth. The 'Babe' was loud, crude, and out-of-control. Gehrig was quiet, polite, and shied-away from making headlines. Manager Miller Huggins preferred

Lou's no-nonsense attitude as it positively affected the entire team, and much unlike Babe Ruth's self-absorbed antics.

Gehrig did not make nearly as much money as Ruth. Gehrig sold life insurance during the off-season, and saved much of it for his parents. Lou did not spend much on cars and jewelry, like so many other young baseball players. Gehrig generally signed the contracts without asking for pay raises, unlike so many other players. In 1927, Babe Ruth was paid $70K, but Gehrig was paid only $8K.

Lou Gehrig exhibited a quiet grace and personal integrity.[120] By 1930, Lou Gehrig held baseball's longest active playing steak at 744 consecutive games. One New York newspaper dubbed, 'Gehrig is certainly one of the Yank's prize locomotive – an Iron Horse.'[121] Gehrig retorted, "This 'Iron Man' stuff is bunk …it is the determination to be in there and to hustle every minute of the time I was there." Gehrig held up well because he took intelligent care, without pampering himself. During his career, he fractured his hands seventeen times, but continued to play.

By the 1930's Babe Ruth and Lou Gehrig were drifting apart. Ruth made fun of his managers, and refused to adopt team rules, i.e., dressing and behaving improperly 'off the field.' Lou Gehrig was just the opposite. On at least one occasion, Gehrig confronted Ruth for his poor off the field behavior. As time went on, Gehrig viewed Babe as a great player, but less than a great man.[122] As Babe Ruth's career was winding down, it was obvious new Yankee manager, Joe McCarty, was building a team around Gehrig, and not around Ruth. By 1935, Babe Ruth had departed the Yankees for the Boston Braves.

After Babe's departure, the vaunted Yankees remained very good. There soon was the addition of another great Yankee outfielder and slugger, Joe DiMaggio. The Gehrig-DiMaggio-led Yankees won four consecutive World Series, in between 1936-39. During his playing career, Lou Gehrig played in seven World Series, and his Yankees won six of them. He was the captain of four straight world's champion teams. In 1936, Lou Gehrig, won the American League's 'Most Valuable Player' for the second time in his career, with 49 homeruns and 152 Runs-Batted-In.

Lou Gehrig had always been seen as a 'Mama's boy.' Lou's mother, Christina, had undue influence, even over his dating. In 1932, Lou rekindled a four-year acquaintance with a Chicago socialite, Eleanor Twitchell. Lou didn't waste any time, and soon proposed. Before the 1933 baseball season was over, Lou and Eleanor wed over his mother's objections. Eleanor widened Lou's life. He began attending, and liking, Broadway plays and ballet. Eleanor exposed Lou to great books and writers. She also believed her husband was selling himself short in the business side of baseball. Marriage agreed with Lou, albeit they were unable to have children.

During the 1938 season, Lou's body began ailing badly. When he made a routine play on a ground ball, three of his teammates remarked, in all sincerity, "Great Stop." Lou realized he was getting undue congratulations for a very ordinary play. Gehrig knew the time had come to quit the game he loved. Given his poor performance during the 1938 season, Gehrig graciously accepted a $3K/year salary cut.[123] Realizing he was not contributing to his club, Lou spoke to his manager, Joe McCarty and decided to hang up his baseball cleats. As team captain in a game in Detroit on May 2, 1939, Gehrig give the line-up card to the home plate umpire without his name on it, the first time in 2,130 games. Gehrig 'benched himself' for the good of the team. Lou Gehrig's baseball playing days were over for good.

A month and a half later, Lou Gehrig was diagnosed with ALS, or Lou Gehrig's Disease. Two weeks later, on July 4, 1939, Gehrig was honored in Yankee Stadium. Babe Ruth even showed up, throwing his arms around Lou. In his farewell speech, before 61,808 Yankee fans, Lou Gehrig, at first, was too choked-up to speak. But then he **delivered**, "Fans, for the past two weeks you have been reading about the bad break I got. Yet today, I consider myself the luckiest man on the face of this earth. I have been in ballparks for seventeen years and have never received anything but kindness and encouragement from you fans. Look at these great men. Which one of you wouldn't consider it the highlight of his career just to associate with them for even one day? Sure, I'm lucky ...When the New York Giants, a team you would give your right arm to beat ...sends you a gift, that's something! When everybody down to the groundskeeper and those boys in white coats remember you with trophies – that's something! …So I close in saying that I may have had a tough break, but I have an awful lot to live for." [124]

Lou did prepare that speech, but he had hoped he would never have to deliver it. He said it was the only time he had ever been frightened on a baseball field. He would have rather struck-out in the ninth inning with the score tied, two down with the bases loaded than deliver this speech. But the crowd kept chanting "We want Gehrig!" And once again Lou Gehrig **delivered**!

More than a half-century later, on September 6, 1995, Cal Ripken Jr. of the Baltimore Orioles broke Lou Gehrig's record playing in his 2,131[st] consecutive game. With his own undeniable class, Cal Ripken responded, "Tonight I stand here, overwhelmed, as my name is linked with the great and courageous Lou Gehrig. I'm truly humbled to have our names spoken in the same breath." Cal Ripken Jr. went on to set the current record at 2,632 consecutive games. When Ripken was a child, he often wore his Little League uniform to bed. Many considered Ripken's playing style a throw-back to that old school game played a half-century earlier.

In early 1940, New York's Mayor, Fiorello LaGuardia, appointed Lou to a position on the city's three-person parole board. Lou Gehrig prepared himself, took the job seriously, and disliked fanfare. But by the spring of 1941, Lou became too weak to even perform his parole board duties.

Looking back, nobody is really sure when Gehrig became afflicted, but many believe it was in early 1938.[125] Amyotrophic Lateral Sclerosis (ALS) is a disease that destroys the covering of the body's nerve fibers. Without this protection, the body's electrical nerve impulses are not properly carried, yet the mind remains alert. As the disease progresses, it consumes the entire body.

June 2, 1941 was the 16th anniversary of the beginning of Lou Gehrig's amazing 14-year game playing streak. This was also the day Lou Gehrig passed-away. His wife Eleanor was at his bedside. She noted "the most beautified expression instantly spread over Lou's face." [126] In keeping with Lou Gehrig's quiet unassuming manner, he did not want a large funeral. It was a small affair, lasting only eight minutes. The Yankees retired Gehrig's Number '4.' This was the first time a professional athlete's number was ever retired.

SOURCES:

Buckley, James, Jr., *Lou Gehrig: Iron Horse of Baseball,'* Sterling Publishing Company, New York, NY, 2010

Burns, Ken and Novick, Lynn, *Baseball,'* DVD, Florentine Films, Walpole, NH and WETA-TV, Washington, D.C., 1994

Greenberger, Robert, *Lou Gehrig,'* The Rosen Publishing Group, New York, NY, 2004

Van Riper, Guernsey, *Lou Gehrig, One of Baseball's Greatest,'* MacMillan Publishing Company, New York, NY, 1949

'Buck' O'Neil

21

'Buck' O'Neil (1911-2006)

...Gracious Ambassador Who Harbored No Resentment

John Jordan 'Buck' O'Neil spent six decades in baseball, as first baseman, coach, manager and scout. Until the day he died, Buck was always the most gracious ambassador for the Negro Leagues, – not to mention a wonderful ambassador for the entire game of baseball!

During his famed Negro League Days, Buck knew and played with nearly every black athlete in the game.[127] Buck had known all of the outstanding Negro League players 'white America' had snubbed, Satchel Paige, Rube Foster, Josh Gibson, Cool Papa Bell, Larry Doby, Jackie Robinson and many others. When the time finally came to tell all Americans, 'the Negro League Story,' Buck O'Neil was their most gracious ambassador. And Buck did it without harboring ill will toward the more privileged white players.

In later years, Buck worked tirelessly to get many Negro League players acknowledged and into Baseball's Hall of Fame. Buck said it meant redemption for Negro League Players to be finally awarded entry into baseball's Hall of Fame. A Hall of Fame induction by a Negro League player was a chance to finally say they were great players. To the living Negro League players it was bigger than immortality; it was an apology.[128]

Rather than dwell on the many injustices he and his fellow Negro League players endured, Buck O'Neil choose to retain the positive memories from his baseball playing and coaching days with the Kansas City Monarchs. This conscious, or perhaps subconscious, decision rendered Buck all that much richer, attracting him to us, whether we were black or white. He taught us to focus on life's positive memories, because negative ones will only weigh us down. Buck's post-baseball playing days of rich memories sustained and uplifted him. In turn, Buck, relating his colorful memories of Baseball's Negro League Days, uplifts us.

Buck's consummate optimism likely came from his grandfather, Julius. Julius was a slave who labored in the Carolina cotton fields. Despite the conditions, Julius still believed the world was an intrinsically good place.

Buck O'Neil was born in Carrabelle, Florida. He joked, "I was born so far south that if I had taken one step backward, I would have been a foreigner." [129] Buck's father was a foreman in the Carrabelle celery-picking fields, and a part-time local baseball player. Buck also worked in the celery fields but did not like it. Buck's father hinted if he wanted to get out of the celery fields, he might consider playing baseball.

Buck moved to Sarasota, Florida. In the 1920's, because of the racially-segregated south, Buck couldn't attend the local high school. In 1934, Buck departed Florida for semi-professional baseball career of 'barnstorming' games. Barnstorming baseball players almost never played home games. Road trips stretched for months on end. Sometimes teams played two or three games during a single day, and in two or three different towns. Players drove through most of the night to arrive at their next day's games. Finding accommodating motels and restaurants, especially in the segregated South, was problematic at best. During the winter months, barnstorming teams would often head to Cuba and Mexico.[130]

Before long, Buck moved-up and was playing in baseball's fast-paced Negro Leagues. The Negro Leagues played a different style of baseball than 'white' baseball. During the 1930's and 40's, in 'white' baseball, it was slugging to get on base, and then more slugging to get the base runners around. In the faster-paced, 'small-ball,' and arguably more exciting Negro Leagues, once a runner reached first base; Watch out! He could steal a base, be bunted over, or something else. A run could be scored without there ever being a hit.[131]

Buck often spoke how wonderful it was to play in the Negro Leagues, and how important it was for those memories to stay alive. Rickety old buses drove players from town to town. Players washed their clothes in cheap hotels, and then dried them off the next day holding them out the bus windows. They ate stale sandwiches. Players were required to use bathrooms and drinking fountains designated for 'coloreds.' People denied their place in America, created their own America. Buck said, "It wasn't a sad time; we overcame." Buck asserted, "we could play, but white folks wouldn't listen."

Buck, and his fellow Negro Leaguers, had every reason to feel cheated by life and time. Buck had been denied so many things, in and out of baseball, because of what he called 'my beautiful tan.' Yet his optimism never failed. Hope never left him. He was always able to find good in people.[132] "Where does bitterness take you? To a broken heart? To an early grave? When I die, I want to die from natural causes. Not from hate eating me up from the inside." [133]

Buck's Kansas City Monarchs were perennially one of best teams in the Negro Leagues. Buck was their hard-hitting first baseman, often hitting stinging line drives. He played a graceful defense at first base. His teammates called him 'Cap,' even when he was young, because he acted like a team captain. Buck knew others players strengths and weaknesses better than they themselves.[134] The Monarchs won five Negro League pennants and two championships. When Buck became their manager, in 1948, and during the waning years of the Negro Leagues, the Monarchs continued winning pennants.

The Monarchs also prided themselves with having class. They wore fitted suits. Their team managers, including Buck, warned local bartenders to cut off players before they drank too much. Players were required to write letters home to their wives every night. Of course, players never gambled. This was especially remarkable in the in 1930's gambling Mecca of Kansas City.[135]

During World War II, Buck broke up his baseball career to serve in the Navy at Subic Bay, Philippines. He was 35 years old when he left the Navy. His first year back into the Negro Leagues, Buck led the League in hitting and was second in hitting the following year.[136] In total, Buck played for 12 years in the Negro Leagues, and eleven of those years with the powerhouse Kansas City Monarchs. His baseball playing statistics

were very good, worthy of consideration into Baseball's Hall of Fame
…when the day would hopefully arrive.

In 1947, and way overdue, Jackie Robinson had to endure many
indignities to become the first black player to break into 'white' baseball
with the Brooklyn Dodgers. But this was also the death knell of Negro
League Baseball. Accepting this reality, Buck O'Neil responded, "But
who cared?"[137]   Later Buck stated, "We are progressing in this country,
[and] Baseball has a lot to do with change in the attitude of people in the
United States.[138]

Buck said "moving is the secret to living" [139] Buck's favorite play was the
triple. Unlike the homerun, where everybody stands around and watches
the ball leave the park, when a triple is hit, or perhaps better said, is
stretched, many players are involved – the hitter, any and all other
possible base runners, as well as many defensive players – outfielders as
well as infielders. The entire playing field bursts into life with a triple.

Buck used to say "It isn't how long you live; it's how well you live." [140]
"If you don't love this game, you'll never be great." [141] "Where does
hate get you?" [142] Buck used to encourage children, "Don't let anyone
tell you, you can't do something. You can do anything and you can be
anyone you want in this world. Remember that." [143]   Buck, who was
never afforded an opportunity to go to high school, could say something
as profound as, "I have learned love and education heal all wounds."

In 1962, with the Negro Leagues long gone, Buck O'Neil was selected as
major league baseball's first black coach, with the Chicago Cubs.
Thereafter, Buck always remained in some sort of capacity with baseball.
White major league star Enos Slaughter, a well-known racist, slid into a
base, purposely slamming his cleats into the first black player in the
major leagues, Jackie Robinson. Buck was then on the veterans
committee to consider Slaughter's worthiness into Baseball's Hall of
Fame. Many folks told Buck not to vote for Slaughter because he was a
racist. Buck responded, "What's that got to do with anything? If we
think like that, we won't let anybody in the Hall of Fame. …Could
[Slaughter] play or couldn't he play? That's what matters."

When asked, "What was the greatest day of his life?" Buck responded, "Easter Sunday, 1943." That day, Buck hit for the rare cycle and also met his future wife, Ora Lee Owens. Ora and Buck never had children. When asked about it, Buck turned it into a joke, saying, "We had a lot of fun trying."

Later Buck and Ora worked hard to establish the Negro League Museum in Kansas City. This museum is Buck's and Ora's child. After Buck returned from the grand opening ceremony in 1997, Buck's wife of 51 years, Ora died in his arms. Ora had been ravaged by cancer. By then, Buck had been to too many funerals and had lost almost all of his friends. Nevertheless, Buck usually found a way to look back at something humorous and laugh.

Every good player dreams of getting an acceptance phone call from Baseball's Hall of Fame. Buck was no different. But that phone call never arrived. Once again, 94-year old Buck O'Neil endured another indignity. Buck may have not been one of the *greatest baseball players*, but he was a very good player. His talents during his 'playing years' are only a small part of the full Buck O'Neil story. He sent more Negro League players into the major leagues than any other manager. Buck was an excellent scout for baseball talent. Late in life, Buck traveled the country promoting, selling, and teaching baseball to children. How could Buck not be voted into Baseball's Hall of Fame class of 2006, while 17 less-deserving players were chosen for the honor? Shame on Baseball!

Buck tried not to show it, but he was heart-broken. He refused to campaign for himself. Many, including this author, seethed with anger at Buck's latest snub. Upon learning of his rebuff, in his always gracious manner, Buck responded, "God's been good to me …Don't weep for Buck. No, man, be happy, be thankful." Buck O'Neil passed away that same year on October 6th.

In Kansas City Royal's Kauffman Baseball Stadium, behind home plate, and in a sea of blue seats, there is one red seat. It's the Buck O'Neil Legacy Seat, awarded to a fan who best exemplifies Buck's Spirit …which thankfully will live on.

SOURCES:

Burns, Ken and Novick, Lynn, *'Baseball'* DVD, Florentine Films, Walpole, NH and WETA-TV, Washington, D.C., 1994

Posnanski, Joe, *'The Soul of Baseball—A Road Trip Through Buck O'Neil's America,'* Harper Collins Publishers, New York, NY, 2007

Ward, Geoffrey and Burns, Ken, *'Baseball—The American Epic—Shadow Ball,'* Alfred A. Knopf, New York, NY, 1994

IV. INSPIRING SERVICE IN DAUNTING TIMES

22

George C. Marshall (1880-1959)

...Farsighted, Dedicated Soldier and Statesman

General George Catlett Marshall was a non-partisan, forthright, selfless public servant our country so desperately needed during the first half of the 20th Century. And this country was incredibly fortunate to have him during most challenging times. During his more than half century public career, George Marshall had staggering responsibilities, serving as Secretary of State, Secretary of Defense, Army Chief of Staff, and International Peace Negotiator. Marshall became one of our nation's, and our world's, most respected leaders. General Marshall had hoped to lead the WW II Allied Invasion on D-Day, June 6, 1944, but President Franklin Roosevelt deemed his leadership in Washington D.C. too important. Instead, this D-Day command generalship was given to General Dwight D. Eisenhower. In fact, Marshall never commanded troops in battle. Today, this is nearly unheard for a high-ranking officer, and most likely would have ended his military career early.

George Marshall was the third and youngest child of George and Laura Marshall, and grew up in a typical middleclass family in Uniontown, Pennsylvania. In school, George was an average student, but excelled in history. He wanted to attend West Point, but his grades were not good enough. The Virginia Military Institute (VMI), a university that provided the Confederate Army with many of its great leaders slightly more than a half century earlier, accepted Marshall as a cadet. During his senior year, Marshall was chosen First Captain. He graduated in 1901.

Because he had graduated from VMI, and not from West Point, there was only a small chance for Marshall to obtain a regular army

George C. Marshall

Dwight D. Eisenhower

commission.   Nevertheless in 1902, Marshall received a regular Army commission.   It took him five years to go from Second Lieutenant to First Lieutenant.   In those pre-World War I days, seniority rather than competency, played a huge role in Army promotions.   Spanish-American War veteran and President, Theodore Roosevelt, began addressing this problem.   Before long, Roosevelt had the very competent John J. Pershing rightfully promoted from Captain to Brigadier General in a span of less than five years.

As the United States was getting involved in World War I, Junior Officer George Marshall encountered General Pershing.   One Day Marshall witnessed Pershing unjustifiably dressing down one of Marshall's fellow junior officers. Unlike everybody else, George Marshall just couldn't let this stand. He spoke up informing Pershing just what he thought of this unjustified outburst.   Many thought Marshall's career was over.   But General Pershing, instead of canning the straight-shooter on the spot, realized this young officer was correct.   Pershing then had George Marshall placed on his own staff.

Marshall had a penchant for clear thinking. He also had a passion for 'wanting to know the facts;' as well as the ability to apply those facts imaginatively. He went to the field himself to collect those facts, and with his diplomatic skills, he was able to implement successful plans and overall strategies. He occasionally tried to obtain combat commands instead of staff work, but his brilliance at staff work was absolutely needed.

During World War I, Marshall was responsible for assisting in the successful designs of military offensives, sometimes involving a million men. As an aide to Pershing, he was said to have a military planning brain, and became an indispensible staff officer.   During that war, Marshall learned to work with Allied leaders such as Winston Churchill. It didn't take long for George Marshall to become well respected among all of the Allied Nations.

After World War I, in 1927, his delicate wife, Lilly, passed away. George Marshall was devastated. Later he went to the Army Infantry School at Fort Benning, Georgia, as Assistant Commandant where he improved infantry tactics. In 1933, Marshall married his second wife, Katherine

Brown. General John Pershing was his best man. During the Great Depression and President Franklin Roosevelt's New Deal, Marshall learned how to work well with local politicians and civilians, especially at Civilian Conservation Corps Camps in Oregon and Washington.

At the beginning of World War II, the country was in dire need of fighting men. The career Army officers in place often overstepped their military regimen on newly-minted 'citizen-soldiers.' Marshall well understood this necessity of a civilian-military dynamic. He was unafraid to correct those professional regular career officers for their callous treatment of the newly minted citizen soldiers.

In 1938, after meeting President Franklin Roosevelt, Brigadier General Marshall remained reserved, while many other dignitaries in the room laughed at his folksy jokes. Marshall was the lone voice of dissent when President Roosevelt presented his poorly conceived plan to send warplanes to Britain. Once again, Marshall opposed his boss. It was assumed his career was over. Instead, Roosevelt appointed Marshall as the Army Chief of Staff. By happenstance, this was the same day World War II was generally acknowledged to have started. On September 1, 1939, Germany blitzed Poland. Within weeks, Germany's Adolf Hitler and Russia's Josef Stalin had carved-up Poland.

Marshall went before Congress, where he had necessary rapport and credibility, asking that institution to preserve the draft. Unlike many, Marshall shunned the spotlight, and had a tendency to step off center stage, letting others receive accolades. After Pearl Harbor, Hawaii was attacked in December 1941, Marshall assured politicians and civilians, "to calm down …we do not need this, but we do need that … and things will work out."

At the start of World War II, the U.S. military, with little modern weaponry, and at only 200,000 troops, was no larger than the army of the Netherlands. It is widely acknowledged Chief of Staff Marshall's successful efforts to build-up our Army to a 10-fold increase by 1942, and then to a 40-fold increase by 1945, loomed huge in the successful outcome of World War II.

General George Marshall took casualty counts seriously. He informed President Roosevelt regularly on casualties. For a while, and before it became too unmanageable, Marshall personally wrote letters to each Gold Star family. Former General Colin Powell stated, "A good leader has to fundamentally rest his or her leadership credentials on the trait of character, and Marshall had that in spades." [144]

Near the war's end, Marshall concurred with President Harry Truman's decision to drop the two atomic bombs on Japan. After the war, President Truman remarked, "Millions gave us extraordinary service, but Marshall gave us victory." In late 1945, and after six years as Chief of Staff, Marshall retired from the Army. The next day President Harry Truman asked Marshall to be Special Ambassador to China and try to mediate a peace deal between Communist Mao Tse-tung and opposing Chiang Kai-shek. Marshall's efforts were less than successful in bringing peace to China.

In 1947, after the Special Ambassador assignment, and against his wife's Katherine wishes, Marshall accepted President Truman's request to become the country's Secretary of State. An extremely vulnerable Europe was becoming more and more unstable. Having first-hand observed the poor handling of the post-World War I world, twenty years prior Marshall and Truman both understood the chain of events that precipitated the second great global war. Marshall declared, "U.S. Interests are best served with an economically strong and stable Europe." Marshall found little support for this idea, and President Harry Truman's approval ratings were very low. The plan Truman and Marshall devised would be called, 'The European Recovery Program,' or 'The Marshall Plan.'

While our country was experiencing its own post-war reconstruction pain and costs, it took much finagling to sell this $13 billion aid plan to Congress, as well as to the American people. This would be the largest economic initiative any nation would take during peacetime. Yet, the Marshall Plan proved to be one of the most far-sighted American actions of the 20th Century. This plan has insured a certain modicum of European Peace ever since.

Between 1948 and 49, Marshall coolly orchestrated the Berlin Airlift that broke a Communist plan to suffocate West Berlin. Marshall resigned from the State Department in 1949. In 1953, George Marshall was awarded the Nobel Peace Prize, for his farsighted efforts in the Marshall Plan to rebuild Europe. Marshall was the only career soldier ever to receive the Nobel Peace Prize.

Despite all his efforts above and beyond patriotic duty, a vitriolic junior senator from Wisconsin slammed George Marshall. He called Marshall a traitor and had charged him with running a State Department full of communists. Remaining dignified, Marshall sighed, "God Bless democracy, I approve of it highly, but I suffer from it extremely." Senator Joseph McCarthy ruined many lives during his four years of induced phobia. McCarthy's early targets were in the State Department and in the Democratic Party. By 1954, journalist Edward R. Murrow began correctly exposing McCarthy as a witch-hunting demagogue.

In 1950, as the Korean War was beginning, President Truman once again tapped the capable Marshall, this time to be his Secretary of Defense. When Marshall responded to President Truman's request, he stated, "I'll do it. But I want you to think about the fact that my appointment may reflect upon you and your administration. They are still charging me with the downfall of Chiang's government in China. I want to help, not hurt you." [145] President Truman, moved by Marshall's perceptiveness and candor, immediately knew Marshall was the best man for this difficult job.

As Secretary of Defense, Marshall once again doubled the Army's size; this time within about six months after the onset of the Korean War. George Marshall was quoted saying, "Military power wins battles, but spiritual power wins wars." Health reasons forced Marshall to resign as Secretary of Defense in 1951.

General George Catlett Marshall passed away in October 1959. Earlier, he had managed General John Pershing's and President Franklin Roosevelt's funerals. For himself, he wanted no large public display, rather just a simple military funeral and burial.

SOURCES:

Cronkite, Walter and Matthau, Walter (narrated by), *'George C. Marshall – The Big Picture,'* You-Tube Video

Pogue, Forrest, *'George C. Marshall: Education of a General, Ordeal of Hope, Organizer of Victory, Statesman,'* Viking Penguin Inc. NY, NY, 1987

Reda, Lou, *'Great Commanders —George C. Marshall: Soldier and Statesman,'* DVD, History Channel Club, A&E Networks, New York, NY, 2005

Harry Truman

Franklin D. Roosevelt

23

Harry Truman (1884-1972)

...Overtaken by Events; But Not Lacking in Decisiveness

It has been said Harry S. Truman was an accidental president. He was also the first U.S. President who had to grab the reins of the office during a major war. President Truman had to, and did, make some of the hardest decisions of the 20th Century. Truman believed a president needed to stick his neck out, rather than be influenced by polls and popular opinion. He believed a president who weighed public opinion first was not well-suited to decide, one way or the other, what was best for the country. In his memoirs he wrote, "To be president of the United States is to be lonely, very lonely at times of great decisions."

Harry Truman also proved to be an extremely hard-working president. In the Oval Office, Truman said, "If a man is acquainted with what other people have experienced at this desk, it will be easier for him to go through similar experiences. It is ignorance that causes most mistakes. The man who sits here ought to know his American history, at least." [146] Truman studied and intimately acquainted himself with the lives of past presidents. He believed by ignoring lessons from the past, the result would be chaos. British Prime Minister Winston Churchill once stated, "Harry Truman, more than any other man, saved western civilization, in the aftermath of World War II."

President Truman made some very tough decisions – dropping two atom bombs, praising the creation of the United Nations and NATO, establishing the Truman Doctrine and the Marshall Plan, organizing the Berlin Airlift, recognizing the state of Israel, and committing American forces on the Korean Peninsula to counter aggression. He also upheld the principle of civilian control over a popular prima donna general, at the cost of his own approval rating.[147] Senator William Proxmire of Wisconsin once said these were all extremely hard 'decisions that many of us would pale before.' In every instance, history, oftentimes many years down the road, proved President Harry Truman made the profoundly difficult but correct decision. When Truman left office in 1953, he was one of the most unpopular presidents in U.S. history, with an approval rating of only 22 percent.

Harry Truman was the only 20th Century President who was unable to go to college. He grew up on a western Missouri farm. His father was often in financial straits, sometimes forced to take second jobs. College for his son was out of the question. Truman was also born with poor eyesight, so he had to wear glasses at a young age. Other children mocked him, calling him 'four eyes.' Bad eyesight also rendered him inept at sports. Hence Harry became an avid reader, and his favorite subject was history.[148]

At school in Independence, Missouri, Harry met Bess Wallace. Harry was immediately smitten. But Bess was from a wealthy family, while Harry was from poorer circumstances. Harry proposed to Bess many times, before she finally relented with a tentative 'Yes.' Harry and Bess finally made wedding plans, but the U.S. entry into World War I got in the way.

In April 1917, President Woodrow Wilson asked Congress to declare war on Germany. Truman decided to do his part. He knew the Army might not accept him on account of his poor eyesight. Hence, he memorized the eye chart. Harry also decided to delay the wedding date until he returned from the war. If he was either killed or maimed in the war, he wanted to spare Bess that burden.[149]

Fighting in Europe, Truman was promoted to First Lieutenant and later to Captain. In command of an artillery battery, his subordinates thought him tough but fair. Near the end of war, Truman's Artillery Battery saw significant action. Only one soldier was lost, and his men placed their low casualty count on Captain Truman's leadership.[150] After the war, Harry Truman returned to Missouri and at last married Bess Wallace. The couple had one child, Margaret.

Back in Missouri, Harry Truman went into a business partnership with Eddie Jacobsen, a Jewish friend he had met in the war. The clothing store, 'Truman and Jacobson Men's Furnishing,' was opened. Initially the store did well. But within two years, Harry and Eddie were forced to close, leaving Truman $12,000 in debt. Truman could have filed for bankruptcy, leaving the store's creditors in a lurch. Believing filing for bankruptcy unethical, Truman paid-off his debt over time. This took two decades.[151]

One of the frequent customers at the store was Jim Pendergast. Jim's uncle was Tom Pendergast.[152] Tom Pendergast controlled the Democratic Party Machine in Kansas City. Tom was the typical, often crooked but powerful local party boss. Tom Pendergast offered Truman an opportunity to enter politics. Initially Truman declined. With the failure of his men's clothing store, Truman accepted Tom Pendergast's offer, and Harry Truman's political career was launched. Truman went into politics because he was a failure at business.[153] Although they were fundamentally opposites, Pendergast liked Truman. Truman was country, emotional and honest; Pendergast was city and unemotional.[154]

In 1922, Harry Truman was elected as County Court Judge, backed by Tom Pendergast's Democratic Party machine. In those days the County Court Judge was not a judicial role, rather an administrative role, somewhat similar to today's county commissioners. As a civic administrator, Truman familiarized himself with the deplorable conditions of the local roads and bridges, and he planned to do something about it. As a county judge, Truman was instrumental in building better local roads as well as reducing the county's debt.[155] Truman proved himself to be incredibly honest. Even his mentor, the corruptible Tom Pendergast couldn't steer Truman toward any tinge of dishonesty. When someone requested a Pendergast favor that didn't sit well with Harry Truman, Pendergast responded, "I told you he was the hardheadedest, orneriest man in the world; there isn't anything I can do."[156] But Tom Penderdgast quietly admired his hard-headed protégé.

After two terms in the position, Harry Truman was ready for a different role in politics, perhaps as a U.S. Congressman from Missouri. Tom Pendergast suggested he run for a U.S. Senate seat from Missouri. As expected, his senatorial opponents charged Truman with being complicit with the Pendergast Machine. Nevertheless Truman's issue-based campaign provided the margin for victory.

In Washington D.C., this new senator was not initially well received and considered a light weight by fellow U.S. Senators. Truman was often labeled 'the Senator from Pendergast,' versus 'from Missouri.' Nonetheless, Truman countered their disdain of him by working harder than ever, typically 12 hours per day.[157] Over time, Truman established himself as a senator who was willing to tackle corruption. He did not flinch from rooting out railroad corruption in his home state of Missouri.[158]

In the meantime, Tom Pendergast's life went downhill. He became a gambling addict, lost money, and accepted more bribes. Soon Pendergast was charged, and sent to prison. Truman's political opponents capitalized on Truman's unwillingness to detach himself from Tom Pendergast. Truman refused to be politically correct and denounce his old friend. Instead, Truman responded, "I'm not a rat who deserts a sinking ship." In 1940, reelection prospects for Senator Truman did not look promising. Nevertheless, in 1940, Harry Truman was re-elected senator from Missouri.

During 1940-41, our country was preparing for war. Defense contractors were blossoming everywhere, making conditions rife for corruption. Fraud and waste were rampant. Senator Truman was placed in charge of the 'Senate Special Committee to Investigate the National Defense Program.' This committee became known as the 'Truman Committee,' and uncovered much fraud and waste, and in turn, saved the American taxpayers around $15 billion.[159]

In 1944, President Franklin Roosevelt was preparing to run for his unprecedented fourth term. Pressures from inside the Democratic Party called for new blood in the selection of Roosevelt's third vice-presidential candidate. The Democrats wanted Roosevelt to choose a moderate, someone between the liberal and conservative factions of their party. That 1944 compromise vice-presidential candidate was Senator Harry Truman. When learning of Truman's selection, Richard Strout of *The New Republic* said, "…Truman is a nice man, an honest man, a good Senator, a man of great humility and a man of courage. He will make a passable Vice President. But Truman as President of the United States in times like these?" [160] To make matters even more challenging for the new Vice President, President Roosevelt kept Truman in the dark concerning major wars plans, including Truman not being apprised of the well underway, but secret Manhattan Project developing the atomic bomb.

In April 1945, Truman had been Vice President for only 82 days when President Roosevelt died. Upon learning of Franklin's Roosevelt death, Truman said to the press corps, "Boys, if you ever pray, pray for me now." Later he said, "I don't know whether you fellows ever had a load of hay fall on you, but when they told me yesterday what happened, I felt like the moon, the stars, and all the planets had fallen on me" [161]

But Truman, the man who had studied so much history, was not without his own well developed and solid views. Truman had a depth of understanding as well as the gravitas to be president. Despite his agrarian Missouri upbringing, Truman was an internationalist. He completely understood the complexity of nations and their interrelationships with one another. Truman was disinclined to bury his head in the sand, or curry to the jingoism of American pride or power.

He knew half of the people in the world were living in conditions of downright misery. For the first time in world history, the knowledge and skills were available to relieve some of that suffering.[162] Truman believed the old imperialist ways of the past, exploiting the poorer less developed countries for a capitalist profit, had no place in the world anymore.

Throughout his life Truman staunchly believed in fairness. When he inherited his predecessor Franklin Roosevelt's 'New Deal' mantle, he gave it his own twist, calling for a 'Fair Deal.' While dealing with the day-to-day annoyances of the job, he later remarked, "…the President is a glorified public relations man who spends his time flattering, kissing and kicking people to get them to do what they are supposed to do anyway." [163]

In early May, slightly less than one month after Truman had taken office, Germany surrendered to the Allies. Nevertheless, Japan remained belligerent, its warlords vowing to fight to the last man. In July 1945, Britain's Winston Churchill, Russia's Joseph Stalin, and President Harry Truman met in Potsdam, Germany to discuss this. These 'Big Three' demanded Japan's surrender. Again Japan remained defiant. Only weeks before, Truman learned of the possible use of a new weapon, the atomic bomb.

Truman's advisors told him if the U.S. were to invade mainland Japan, the Japanese would greatly resist. The fighting would be horrific, and American casualties could reach 500,000 before an American victory could be realized.[164] But there was another possible option to end the war, that ominous weapon, the atomic bomb. On July 2, 1945 once again Japan was advised to surrender; Japan refused. By the end of the month Truman authorized the use of the atomic bomb. On August 6, 1945, the first atom bomb was dropped on the Japanese city of Hiroshima; 80,000 Japanese died instantly and another 50,000-60,000 would later lose their lives.[165] But the Japanese still would not surrender. Three days later, on August 9, 1945, a second atom bomb was dropped on Nagasaki. That day, Nagasaki was the alternate target city, due to poor visibility over the primary target city of Kokura. Kokura was spared and Nagasaki was hit. In Nagasaki, 70,000 Japanese immediately perished.[166] Within the week, the Japanese finally agreed to surrender. World War II would soon be declared be over!

President Truman, alone, made the decision to drop the atomic bomb, and it was probably one of the most difficult made by any president in the 20th Century. He knew beforehand it would instantly kill tens of thousands of Japanese. On the other hand, a protracted war would have cost 500,000 or more American lives; not to mention the hundreds of thousands of Japanese lives, had an invasion of the Japanese mainland taken place.

With World War II over, domestic quarreling between labor and management began anew in America.[167] Labor demanded pay hikes to make up for wages lost during the war, and to counter the threat of inflation. When management did not comply, labor unions went on strike. Before long the U.S. steel-producing industry was at a standstill. Coal and railroads workers also went on strike, crippling the entire national railroad system. Strikes paralyzed the country. While Truman had a record of supporting the unions, he strongly disapproved of the many strikes. Hence, President Truman took a tough stance against the unions. But he paid a price for it. Labor Unions, who once thought of

Truman as a friend, 'unfriended' him, and voted against his Democratic Party. During the mid-term elections of 1946, the Democrats were badly beaten because of Truman's personal unpopularity, which had dropped from 87 percent to 32 percent.[168]

After the World War II, the relationship between allies of the United States and Stalin's Russia soured. Before long, Russia had set up puppet communist governments in the countries of Eastern Europe. Germany was divided in two. East Germany fell into the Soviet sphere of influence. President Truman became convinced he had to contain the spread of totalitarian Communist regimes. To this effect, in March 1947, Truman championed his 'Truman Doctrine.' It stated the U.S. would support any nation that could potentially fall under a Communist regime. This doctrine was especially intended for vulnerable small countries. During this time, Greece and Turkey were close to falling under Soviet rule. The U.S. sending aid to Greece and Turkey may very well have prevented these two, now E.U. member countries, from becoming communist countries.

The continued aid from the U.S. to a badly weakened post-World War II Europe evolved into the 'European Recovery Program,' later known as 'The Marshall Plan.' Truman and his farsighted Secretary of State, George Marshall, grasped the importance of Europe needing to be economically healthy and viable. After World War II, it was unpopular to divert U.S. dollars to help Europe, with all of the problems at home. But Truman and Marshall correctly foresaw it was necessary for world peace. Truman, by way of George Marshall, convinced Congress to spend $13 billion to help rebuild Western Europe.

Before long, non-communist West Berlin, located in communist East Germany became isolated from overland rail and truck support coming from non-communist West Germany. Truman could have relented, allowing the Soviets both East and West Berlin, or Truman could have risked war with the Soviets. Instead Truman and his advisors came up with the Berlin Airlift. Military cargo planes would deliver, on a massive scale, badly needed supplies, food, coal, and other necessities to the people of West Berlin. Nothing like this had ever been attempted before. The airlift was a success. After about a year of the airlift, realizing the futility of their ground blockade, the Soviets again granted ground access to West Berlin. West Berlin was to remain a free and capitalistic city.

In the spring of 1948, people thought Harry Truman was incapable of winning in the November General Election. His approval rating was around 36 percent. Even the Democratic Party was unsure about having an incumbent president at the top of their ticket. Nevertheless, with some worry, the Democrats selected Harry Truman as their presidential candidate.

Throwing political correctness aside, Truman continued to ruffle the Democrats when he pushed to improve civil rights. The Dixiecrat Branch of the Democratic Party did not want more civil rights. When Truman affirmed his commitment to civil rights, many Dixiecrats simply walked out of the 1948 Philadelphia Democratic Convention.[169]

Within weeks of the Philadelphia convention, President Truman issued executive orders integrating the military and civil service, further infuriating the Dixiecrats. In 1948 general election, President Truman ran against both Republican Thomas Dewey and Dixiecrat Strom Thurmond. During that election run, Truman undertook an energetic 20,000-mile whistle-stop train campaign across the country. He portrayed himself as 'the little guy,' who he truly was, running against established 'giants.' Truman stunned the nation when he was elected president, and this time in his own right.

In April 1949, even with the success of the Berlin Airlift, the communist threat to Western Europe was still very real. Truman, his Secretary of State and the British Foreign Secretary devised a countering plan. That plan stated if a communist country, and at that time there were several in Eastern Europe, were to attack any democratic western European country, all twelve of the signatories to this new treaty considered it attack on 'All.' The signatories to this mostly-western European agreement, plus the U.S. and Canada, became the North Atlantic Treaty Organization (NATO). Joining NATO was popular with the U.S. Senate who easily passed legislation admitting the United States. Truman selected General Dwight D. Eisenhower as the first Allied

Commander of NATO. The security benefits nations derived from being NATO members have far outlived President Truman.

Truman always had an interest in the history of the Middle East. After World War II, he called for a homeland for those Jews who survived Nazi horrors. Middle Eastern Arabs were opposed to a Jewish state in their region, an area long populated by Arabs. Early on, many State Department officials, not wishing to offend the Arabs, discouraged the idea of establishing a Jewish homeland in the Middle East. Some in the government, including his Secretary of Defense, warned President Truman of the likely importance of Saudi Arabian oil in the event of another war. President Truman countered he would handle the situation in the light of justice, not oil.[170]

Korea had been occupied by Imperial Japan for about 35 years, before World War II. At the end of World War II, Korea was split in two. The Soviets gained control of Korea north of the 38th Parallel, while the U.S. and Allies maintained control south of the 38th Parallel. In June 1950, communist North Korea surprised and invaded non-communist South Korea by crossing the 38th Parallel. After two months in faltering defense, the South Korean forces were pushed into the southeastern corner of the country, near Pusan. Truman knew the South Koreans did not have the strength to repel an invasion from North Korea. Truman felt the U.S. should not stand by and watch a lightly-armed country be taken over by the communist aggressors, North Korea and its allies, Russia and China.

Within months, famed World War II icon, General Douglass MacArthur, landed his forces at Inchon, on South Korea's western coast on the Yellow Sea. Inchon was not too far south of the 38th Parallel, and near the capitol city of Seoul. MacArthur's troops were successful at isolating, neutralizing, and forcing the North Korean aggressors back over the 38th Parallel. President Truman approved MacArthur crossing the 38th Parallel pursuing North Korean soldiers. However, MacArthur wanted to do even more, and push farther north across the Yalu River, beyond the border of North Korea, and into China.

In the meantime North Korea's Communist Allies, Russia and China were now collaborating to help beleaguered North Korea. Russia was providing air support, while China entered the conflict providing soldiers. When well-armed China entered the conflict, non-Communist United Nations forces were pushed backed, and southwards. Once again, and for a second time, the South Korean Capital of Seoul was occupied, this time largely by Chinese Communists.

Facing this quandary, General MacArthur wanted to escalate the war and have his own prerogative on whether or not to use nuclear weapons, even if used against the Chinese. China also had nuclear weapons, and Truman surely did not want to start a nuclear holocaust. By April 1951, the confrontational, albeit popular, General MacArthur left President Truman with no other choice but to relieve him. MacArthur returned to the States, and was given a hero's welcome, including a ticker-tape parade through the streets of New York City. MacArthur spoke to a Joint Session of Congress panning President Truman. Truman's popularity plummeted to 22 percent. This was the lowest Gallup Poll approval rating recorded by any serving president. Nevertheless, in retrospect most historians agree the unpopular Truman made the correct decision by dismissing the celebrated but troublesome general.

With the clarion call up to be on guard for worldwide communist aggression, one freshman Republican Senator from Wisconsin was all too willing to ingratiate himself with more power. Senator Joseph McCarthy stoked fear in the country and made unfounded, but unfortunately believable, cases there were communist agents hiding around every corner.[171] McCarthy was having his heyday after Truman relieved MacArthur. No doubt any *real* communists loved this fearsome portrayal of their over-blown influence in the U.S. Witch-hunting McCarthy ruined many lives by accusing people in government and public life they were Communist, when they weren't. Truman's Secretary of Agriculture had found dirt on McCarthy, including McCarthy's extramarital affairs. He informed President Truman of such, and as a way to get back at McCarthy for his dirty tricks. Truman would not approve of this justified retaliation saying, "Nobody, not even the President of the United States, can approach too close to a skunk, in skunk territory, and expect to get anything out of it except a bad smell." [172]

In his early political years, some Truman detractors stated he probably made some less-than-fully-moral compromises on Civil Rights. But so did Abraham Lincoln, sixty years earlier. However, in the late 1930's, during his first term as a U.S. Senator from Missouri, Truman had taken positions that belied his Southern background. He supported the position to abolish poll taxes, as well as supported legislation to combat Southern lynching. He used presidential authority to begin racial integration of the military and federal agencies. He made civil rights part of the national political agenda.

During the Korean War, President Truman learned a Native American soldier, who was killed in action, was not permitted to be interred in his local Iowa cemetery because he was not Caucasian. This enraged Truman. He saw to it that this soldier was to be buried at Arlington National Cemetery, and an Air Force plane was sent to pick up his casket, widow and three children.[173]

At the end of his presidency, Truman was unpopular with an approval rating as low as 32 percent. Truman took little stock in polls, but instead tried 'to do right' by history. When asked about those very unfavorable poll numbers, Truman responded, "I wonder how far Moses would have gone if he'd taken a poll in Egypt? ...What would Jesus Christ have preached if he'd taken a poll in Israel? ...It isn't polls or public opinion of the moment that counts. It's right and wrong." [174]

Reflecting on Truman's Presidency, historian Allan Nevins said, "...his penetrating shrewdness has been underrated...In ordinary affairs he seemed commonplace, and in small matters he could make curious blunders. But he grew in his office as few Presidents have ever done; and he was sustained by an unusual knowledge of American history and a firm grasp of our best traditions. To the major crisis he brought statesmanship-like insight, energy, and courage. There was a greatness in the man..." [175]

When Truman departed the White House on January 20, 1953, Harry and Bess simply took a train back to Independence, Missouri. They quickly settled into his old family home. Truman was not wealthy before he became president, and much like Ulysses Grant, when he finished his presidency, Truman remained far from wealthy.

Many companies and organizations were willing to pay the ex-president for endorsements and political lobbying. Truman declined most of these offers as he wished to engage in projects he considered more legitimate.[176] Like Ulysses Grant, Truman was approached and offered to be paid for stories from his perspective. Like Grant, Truman was warm to the idea, and his writings provided his family with a small degree of financial salvation.

At a white-tie dinner in London, Lord Halifax paid the elderly Truman an interesting compliment, "I think we in this room feel that you are the sort of chap with whom all of us would be quite happy to go tiger hunting." [177] Once a reporter asked Truman whether he considered himself the sublimation of the average man, Truman rejected such fancy phraseology and asked the reporter, "Well, what is wrong with being the average man?" [178]

Harry Truman never tried to appear as something he was not. He came directly from the people. He was the kind of president our Founding Fathers had in mind.[179] In 1948, George Marshall said it was "The integrity of the man." [180]

In a post-presidential interview, Truman said, "Three things corrupt a man – power, money and women. I never had but one woman in my life, and she's right at home. I never wanted power, and I never had any money, so I don't miss it." Perhaps Truman's greatest legacy was proving a common person could **succeed** as President. He did so by being himself.[181]

When Harry Truman passed-away in December 1972, Bess Truman opted for a simple private service at the Truman Library, versus a state funeral in Washington, D.C. Many offered tributes, "He was not a hero or a magician...He was a certifiable member of the human race, direct, fallible, and unexpectedly wise when it counted ...He did not require to be loved. He did not expect to be followed blindly. Congressional opposition never struck him as subversive, nor did he regard his critics as traitors. He never whined. He did not blame reporters for his failures. He did not use the office as a club or a shield, or as a hiding place. He worked at it … He said he lived by the bible and history." [182]

Over time, and looking back through the more dependable lens of history, the unpopular President Truman, upon his departure in 1953, has been consistently rated by recent historians as one of the top 10 greatest Presidents in our history.[183]

SOURCES:

Mara, Wil, *'Harry Truman – Presidents and Their Times,'* Marshall Cavendish Corporation,' Tarrytown, NY, 2012

McCullough, David, *'Truman,'* Simon and Schuster, New York, NY, 1992

Schuman, Michael A. *'Harry S. Truman,'* Enslow Publishers, Inc. Springfield, NJ, 1997

Tullai, Martin, *'Presidential Standouts'* 'The Elks Magazine, May 2016

Louis Zamperini

24

Louis Zamperini (1917-2014)

...Survival and Forgiveness

In Torrance, California, Louis Zamperini was fast on his feet – real fast. Louie was a track star at the University of Southern California. In 1936, he even made the U.S. Olympic team going to Berlin. At the Olympics, he finished eighth in the 5,000-meter race, with a super-fast final lap, that caught the attention of the German Chancellor, Adolf Hitler. After that amazing long-distance finish, Hitler sought an audience with Louie.

\-

In 1941, Zamperini joined our war effort and was commissioned a Second Lieutenant in the U.S. Army Air Corps. In the Pacific Theatre, he served as the bombardier aboard two B-24 Liberators. The second plane, the *Green Hornet*, and already been cannibalized for parts. Nevertheless, it was still used for search and rescue missions. In May, 1943, the lumbering *Green Hornet* crashed into the Pacific Ocean about 850 miles south of Oahu, Hawaii. Zamperini and only two others initially survived the crash. Their real troubles were just beginning. The eventual two survivors endured 47 days in a leaky life raft. Famished, they were threatened by sharks and strafed several times by Japanese war planes. When Louie and the other surviving life raft crew member, Russell Phillips, made landfall, it was on the Japanese-held Marshall Islands. Things were about to get horribly worse.

'Zamp' and 'Phil' were captured and made Prisoners of War. After 42 days, they were shuttled from a POW camp in the Pacific to one on mainland Japan. Things turned unbearable. For two years, held in three harsh prison camps, Louie endured merciless and unspeakable torture. One Japanese guard in particular, a Corporal, named 'the Bird,' was especially sadistic.

It's amazing anyone could survive these extreme tortures, but 'unbroken' Lieutenant Louis Zamperini did! By the summer of 1945, thanks to successful B-29 aircraft bombing raids, Japan was clearly losing the war and its citizens were suffering badly. The American and Allied Prisoners of War, held on mainland Japan, were likely to be murdered, in part, because the Japanese military wanted no breathing witnesses to their POW war crime atrocities. By early September 1945, and after those two atomic bombs fell, the stunned Japanese didn't know what to do. The security around Japanese POW camps dissolved. Soon Lieutenant Zamperini and possibly as many as 90,000 former American and Allied POWs inside Japan found their way to friendly Allied forces ...and to freedom!

After the war, and not far behind the ruthless Japanese War Lord Hideki Tojo, 'the Bird' was near the top of 'the most wanted list' for his war crimes. But for nearly seven years, 'the Bird' was able to elude authorities. In 1952, the Japanese, and even the American, appetite for hunting down war criminals had dried up. When that happened, 'the Bird' resurfaced, married, had two children, and opened a profitable insurance agency in Tokyo.

After the War, things didn't go as well for traumatized Louie Zamperini. He married, but fell into alcohol abuse and other post-traumatic stress disorder (PTSD). He often awoke screaming with nightmares. And he was obsessed to take out his due vengeance on 'the Bird.'

In 1949, with the coaxing of his wife Cynthia, Louie Zamperini attended a Billy Graham Revival in Los Angeles. It got him thinking, "Could I ever forgive the Bird?" Over time, this man of so much courage and perseverance found it in his heart to forgive even 'the Bird.' The war was over for Louie!

By 1952, Louis found a calling helping troubled youths. As a rambunctious youth himself, he often looked for thrills. Louis had insights where these kids were coming from. He thought an effort to divert them from a life of crime to adrenaline-filled wilderness adventures, like glacier climbing and rappelling, might just work. At the evening campfires, after an exhilarating day outdoors, Louis got many troubled youths to open up. Not surprisingly, he learned these at risk youths lacked respect for themselves and for others. In a no pressure approach, Louis relayed how God's healing love and forgiveness had saved him after the war. Many at-risk youths, bought into Louis' heart-felt message of 'survival and forgiveness.' Young lives were changed. The non-profit Victory Boys Camp was started outside Los Angeles. This effort continues to this day as the Louis Zamperini Foundation (www.louiszamperinifoundation.org).

Louis Zamperini would run in the Olympics again. At the 1984 Summer Olympics in Los Angeles, former Olympic runner, Louie Zamperini was given the honor to carry the Olympic torch! Fourteen years later, at the 1998 Winter Olympics in Nagano, Japan, and not far from where he was held as a Prisoner of War over a half-century earlier, a frail, 80-year old Louie was offered this same torch-carrying honor, before a sea of smiling Japanese faces!

After that, this wonderful man sought out his former tormentor, 'the Bird,' to express that healing forgiveness. But 'the Bird' practically spat on Zamperini's letter, replying, "No." 'The Bird' died five years later in 2003.

SOURCE:
Hillenbrand, Laura, *"Unbroken,"* Random House, New York, NY, 2010

Chief Joseph Medicine Crow

25

Joseph Medicine Crow (1913-2016)

...Heroics in War and in Peace

The Crow Nation started out as Woodland Native Americans in the Ohio area. They were pushed further and further west by white men and other Native Americans, until they got a toehold in the Montana-Wyoming-Yellowstone River region. By the 1870's, the Crow Indians were often victimized by other Northern Plains Indians. Neighboring Blackfeet, Cheyenne, and Sioux were territorial and warlike, and often attacked the Crow. So, allying themselves with the white man made a degree of sense to the Crow.

In 1876, Joseph Medicine Crow's grandfather, was a Crow scout for General George Armstrong Custer. Young Joseph Medicine looked up to and was inspired by his grandfather in the finest of Crow warrior traditions. As an eyewitness to The Battle of Little Big Horn, Joseph Medicine Crow's grandfather often relayed this Native American victory to his young grandson.

Arrogant and blindly driven to kill Plains Indians, Custer caused the obliteration of five of his twelve 7th Cavalry companies, or 268 men, in the Battle of Little Big Horn on June 25, 1876. Counter to the advice of his mostly Crow Scouts, Custer and his men planned to attack a much larger combined force of Lakota, Northern Cheyenne, and Arapaho. Unlike their leader Custer, his Crow Scouts were convinced they were all doomed to die in the forthcoming battle. Hence, Joseph Medicine Crow's grandfather and fellow Indian Scouts doffed their Seventh Cavalry uniforms and donned their Crow war clothing. An angry Custer demanded to know why. The scouts responded they would rather die as warriors than die as U.S. Soldiers.

Young Joseph Medicine Crow loved to learn and strove to become educated. Before World War II, he started out at a Baptist Mission

School and earned a degree in sociology. In 1943, he interrupted his graduate schooling to join the U.S. Army. After the war, he earned his Masters Degree in anthropology from University of Southern California, and was the first of his Crow Nation to acquire a Masters Degree. Years later, an elder Joseph Medicine Crow was presented with an honorary doctorate.

During World War II, Medicine Crow was assigned as a scout in Europe. His only goal was to be a good soldier and perform honorably in combat.[184] But before going into battle, under his uniform, he wore red war paint on his arms and an eagle feather inside his helmet. The days of Plains Indians 'counting coup,' or attaining 'war deeds' were long gone. Nevertheless, the Crow and many other Plains Indians held a centuries-honored tradition: How to become a 'War Chief.' A Crow warrior must perform four dangerous deeds. These acts of bravery were: 1) Lead a successful war party; 2) Take an enemy's weapon; 3) Touch an enemy without killing him; and 4) Steal an enemy's horse. Unbelievably, and never planning to, Joseph Medicine Crow accomplished all four of these feats during World War II!

In France, Joseph Medicine Crow led six men across exposed no-man's-land subject to German land mines, and mortar and gunfire. Their mission was to retrieve boxes of dynamite stored near the French Maginot Line. Their only cover was the smoke screen projectiles launched by the Americans behind them. In the smoke, this patrol had to run crouched close to the ground, so they could spot the tiny flags Army Engineers had previously planted to mark known land mines. Stepping on an unseen or an unmarked land mine would be lethal. Incredibly, all seven men were able to safely return to the friendly line, with each soldier carrying a retrieved 50-pound box of dynamite! That dynamite was later used to successfully blow up German pillboxes and guns. Not realizing it, Joseph Medicine Crow had just accomplished his first war deed.

Two months later, while a main American force was attacking a German-occupied French village, scout Joseph Medicine Crow was to sneak into the village from the opposite direction, and make an assessment and a report on German troop and artillery strength.[185]

Medicine Crow entered the rear of the village without being noticed. However, darting along, he bumped head-on into a German soldier bigger than himself. With his quick reactions, he was able to dislodge the German's rifle. Hand to hand combat ensued. Eventually, in this life-or-death match, Joseph Medicine Crow got the better of the German. Crow was about to choke and kill the man, when the German soldier moaned, "Mama, Mama." Joseph Medicine Crow says his ears were opened, and without much thought, he released his death-grip on the German. Medicine Crow was able to flee the scene before more Germans were able to investigate the noise coming from the unseen commotion. Again, and not recognizing it, Medicine Crow attained two more war deeds, knocking down an enemy, and disarming him.

Close to the end of the war, Medicine Crow's unit was stealthily tracking about 50 of Hitler's SS Officers, who were on horseback.[186] Settling in for the night at a farmhouse, the SS Officers left their horses in an enclosed fenced pasture. Medicine Crow, an excellent horseman since his youth, suggested to his captain, he sneak into the pasture in order to get the horses to stampede. The captain agreed to this brazen plan. In the darkness, Medicine Crow and one other soldier silently crept past the farmhouse guards. His fellow soldier was to open the fence's gate on a soft whistle signal from Medicine Crow. Without spooking the horses in the enclosure, Medicine Crow found a horse he liked. He softly fastened a Crow-style, hand-made rope bridle onto the horse, and mounted it. Medicine Crow then sounded that soft whistle signal to let his compatriot working the gate know he was ready. The stampede was on!

Medicine Crow recounted with a laugh, "I got on it, rounded up the other horses and stampeded them out of there, giving a Crow war cry." [187] After that audacious feat, with bullets whizzing behind him, Medicine Crow knew his grandfather and his other ancestors were very proud of him! But he still didn't comprehend the significance of his fourth brave deed. For his bravery during the war, Chief Joseph Medicine Crow received the Bronze Star and the French Legion of Honor.

When Crow soldiers returned from World War II, a grand reception with dancing and drums was held in their honor. Among other festivities and accounts, Medicine Crow was obliged to recount his experiences as an American soldier fighting in Europe. When he finished with his recitation, his elders declared, "You have done it! You have done the four deeds! You are a War Chief!" Hence, Chief Joseph Medicine Crow became the *Last* Plains Indian War Chief!

After the war, Chief Joseph Medicine Crow remained dedicated to his Crow people. He served as the tribal spokesman, anthropologist, and tribal historian for more than 50 years. He saw his people's efforts to preserve their traditions and languages as a good thing, and not something the government should try to outlaw or forbid, as it had often tried to do in the past. He used his deserving War Chief influence to champion rights for his Crow people.[188] What a great role model for his people, as well as for all Americans!

SOURCES:
Burns, Ken, and Novick, Lynn *'The War,'* Florentine Films,
     Walpole, NH, 2007
Law, Steven, *The Last Plains Indian War Chief still fights for his home,
     his people and their way of life,'* The Deseret News, Salt Lake City, UT,
     Dec 6, 2012

26

Daniel Inouye (1924-2012)

...Unwavering Service to his Country

Young Daniel Inouye's father and mother were from Japan. Daniel Inouye was known as a 'Nisci' – American born to Japanese immigrating parents. Daniel was just 17 years old when his city Honolulu, Hawaii, was bombed on December 7, 1941. Looking up and seeing the red rising sun on the attacking warplanes, Daniel said something like "Oh, Oh, I know what's happening here; my world has just come to an end." He correctly figured that there would be adverse repercussions on Japanese-Americans living in the United States. Most of these Japanese-Americans were living along the West Coast and in the U.S. Territory of Hawaii. There certainly were awful repercussions for these unfortunate Americans.

Young Daniel Inouye had hoped to become a doctor. As a Red Cross Volunteer, during the awful attack on Pearl Harbor, Daniel Inouye witnessed horrible sights. Some of those memories haunted him for the rest of his life.

On December 7th, Pearl Harbor lost eight battleships, 164 aircraft and 2,403 un-expecting souls. Less than six weeks after Pearl Harbor, President Franklin Roosevelt issued an Executive Order rounding-up about 120,000 of Japanese ancestry, 11,000 of German and 3,000 of Italian ancestry. About 70,000 of these with Japanese ancestry were American citizens. The other 50,000 or so non-Americans citizens of Japanese extraction had been living in the United for 20-40 years. Yet, racist fear-mongering overtook the country. Could this ever happen again in the 21st Century? No solid evidence was ever found implicating disloyalty by any America Nisei or other Japanese-Americans. Yet, these Americans typically lost their homes, their businesses, and their lands.

The internment camps these people were sent to consisted of tar-paper shacks with little heat in the winter, or cooling in the summer. They were

Daniel Inouye

guarded by soldiers and surrounded by barbed wire. Nisei and Japanese-Americans on Hawaii suffered less than their counterparts located on the U.S. mainland. This was because it would have been impractical and too unwieldy to move such a large number of detainees, and over one-third of Hawaii's population, to U.S. mainland internment camps. Furthermore, the Hawaiian economy would have collapsed with their removal.

These wronged Americans of Japanese ancestry incarcerated in mainland internment camps and those in Hawaii wanted to prove their loyalty to America. By early 1943, the U.S. War Department authorized the 442nd Regimental Combat Team, consisting of Americans of Japanese ancestry. However, this unit was only allowed to fight in Europe, not in the Pacific Theater.

In 1944, the 442nd landed in Italy. They moved through Italy, southern France, and Germany. In the Vosges Mountains of France, the 442nd rescued an isolated Texas National Guard Battalion, known as the 'Lost Battalion.' Before long, the 442nd became the most decorated unit, for their size, in American warfare, with a casualty rate of 2.5 times their initial number. Replacements were always coming in. The 442nd was awarded eight Presidential Unit Citations. Twenty one soldiers were awarded Congressional Medal of Honors, along with nearly 10,000 Purple Hearts. Don't ever tell this author that this brave unit had any disloyal Americans!

In 1943, soon after its formation, 18-year old Daniel Inouye cut-short his college education in medicine to join the 442nd. He was soon promoted to sergeant, later to platoon sergeant, and then to lieutenant. Leading one attack, he was shot in the chest, but the bullet struck two 'lucky' silver dollars in his shirt pocket, allowing Daniel live and fight on.

Less than three weeks before the War in Europe was officially over, hard-charging Second Lieutenant Daniel Inouye's actions later merited him the Congressional Medal of Honor in Italy's Po Valley. While Inouye and his unit were approaching a ridge, about 40 yards distant, they were pinned-down by three German machine gun nests. Even though, he was wounded in the stomach and leg, and losing much blood, Inouye continued assaulting the Germans, throwing grenades into two of the three German machine gun nests. By the time he was about to heave a grenade into the third nest, German gunfire wounded and immobilized his grenade-throwing right arm and hand. Lieutenant Inouye's cocked and helpless right arm was non-functional while holding a live grenade! His men approached, wanting to help him. He ordered them back, fearing if the grip on his grenade hand lapsed, all near him would perish. With his functioning left hand, he was able to pry the grenade from his useless right hand, and then successfully pitch it into the third machine gun nest just in the nick of time. Then Lieutenant Inouye fell to the ground unconscious. In his gallantly lead attack, 25 German soldiers were killed and another eight were captured.

Without sufficient anesthesia, military surgeons had to removed Lieutenant Daniel Inouye mutilated right arm. He needed 17 blood transfusions. These 17 transfusions came from soldiers in an African American unit. Inouye remarked he was never so happy to receive this wonderful gift from these African-Americans. Daniel Inouye spent nearly two years in Army Hospitals recovering. In one European Army Hospital, Inouye met another badly wounded young officer who had also lost the use of his right arm, Bob Dole. Within a couple decades, Democrat Daniel Inouye and Republican Bob Dole were working together in the U.S. Senate.

Leaving the Army, without a right arm, Inouye's dream of becoming a surgeon was crushed. Instead, he furthered his education under the GI Bill, studying political science and law. He was soon elected to the legislature serving his native territory of Hawaii. In 1959, when Hawaii became our 50th state, Daniel Inouye became its first elected Congressman. Three years later, Daniel Inouye was elected a U.S. Senator from Hawaii, where he served for 50 years with distinction. During his fruitful Senate career, he chaired many vital Senate Committees. He was a voice for moderation as well as for curtailing excesses in government. Late during his political career, Senator Daniel Inouye cautioned Americans, "I hope that the mistakes made, and suffering imposed upon Japanese-Americans nearly 60 years ago will not be repeated against Arab-Americans whose loyalties are now being called into question."

In 2018, a Navy Destroyer, due for launching from Bath Iron Works in Maine, will be christened the USS Daniel Inouye.

\-

SOURCES:

Associated Press (Chicago), *'Keynoter Knows Sting of Bias, Poverty,'*
    St. Petersburg Times, August 27, 1968
Burns, Ken, and Novick, Lynn *'The War,'* Florentine Films,
    Walpole, NH, 2007
Susan Sinnott, *'Extraordinary Asian Americans and Pacific Islanders,'*
    Children's Press, New York, NY, 2003

Vivien Thomas

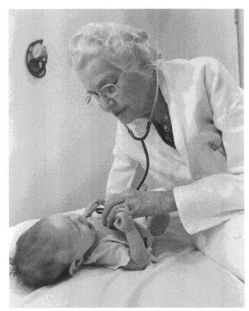

Helen Taussig

Alfred Blalock

VI. CONTRIBUTING IN A BEFUDDLED WORLD

27

Vivien Thomas (1910-1985)
...The Genius Working in the Shadows

In 1912, William Thomas, a skilled black carpenter, moved his family, his wife Mary and their four boys, from Louisiana to Nashville, Tennessee. William and Mary's fourth son, Vivien, followed his father's footsteps and became a capable carpenter. But young Vivien had even bigger dreams. He wanted to become a doctor. During the 1930's, this dream was not all that outrageous even for a young black man in the segregated south. In Nashville, Vivien earned relatively good money. He socked it away, and graduated from his high school with honors.

In 1930, as our Great Depression was beginning, the bank where Vivien had been placing dollars for his future medical education shuttered. Every dollar Vivien had saved during seven years of carpentry work was gone. Vivien was out of school and now out of work.

Dr. Alfred Blalock was already a well-known doctor, coming from a prestigious family in Georgia. In 1922, Blalock graduated from Baltimore's John Hopkins University. In 1925, he accepted a position at Nashville's Vanderbilt University. In 1930, when Vivien Thomas approached Blalock, looking for a job, Blalock saw promise in the young black man. Blalock needed a competent lab assistant, and decided Thomas was to be his lab man. However, Blalock had to categorize Thomas' job, and his earnings, as a janitor, because Thomas was a black man.

Early in their relationship, the short-tempered Blalock unreasonably exploded on Vivien Thomas. As much as Vivien needed a job, he would not stand for this verbal abuse. Vivien Thomas stood up to Dr. Blalock. Blalock promised he would never treat his lab technician like

179

that again. Blalock was true to his word, and kept the promise. Both men grew to appreciate each other more and more. However, outside the laboratory, they lived in separate segregated worlds.

Soon Blalock and Thomas were working on experiments relating to life-threatening circulatory shock and cardiac output. Doctor Blalock came to the unconventional conclusion shock was caused by lack of blood and other vital body fluids. That research saved hundreds of lives on the battlefields of World War II. Associated with this research, the importance of the availability of blood plasma became paramount.

In 1941, with Alfred Blalock gaining prominence, he was offered a position at his alma mater, John Hopkins University, where he was to be chief of surgery. Blalock didn't waste any time requesting his right-hand-man, his lab assistant 'janitor,' Vivien Thomas, also be hired at John Hopkins. Vivien and Clara Thomas and their growing family had some reservations about moving out of the house Vivien had built in Nashville to move to Baltimore. The Blalock's arrived in Baltimore with fanfare. But the Thomas family found an even more stratified and segregated society than the one they had left in Nashville.

In 1943, a fellow pioneer and child cardiologist at John Hopkins, Helen Taussig, approached Blalock and Thomas about a condition that was killing thousands of babies and young children every year, 'The Blue Baby Syndrome.' A symptom of this was many of the babies' extremities, lips, fingers, and feet, turned blue. These limbs were not getting enough oxygenated blood. Healthy babies receive much more oxygen to their extremities, and this is manifested by a healthy rosy color, such as red lips.

The heart pumps blood to the lungs where it is enriched with oxygen. After receiving oxygen from the lungs, blood turns from bluish to reddish. If the lungs do not receive enough blood, less oxygenated blood is pumped back into other body systems. This lack of oxygenated blood manifests itself in an unhealthy bluish, versus reddish, color that is most evident in the extremities. How can so small a heart pump more blood into the lungs? Do some plumbing work on the human heart? This was a very unorthodox idea. In the early 1940's, heart surgery was taboo. At the time, it was accepted that doctors should not alter a beating heart. But yet, there was the potential to save countless babies' and young children's lives.

Vivien Thomas went to work. He designed and made his own tiny instruments. He humanely operated on dogs with the condition. After Vivien Thomas performed about 200 such dog operations, he perfected the procedure. Finally, a dog named Anna, once sick, became healthy. A picture of Anna is the only animal photograph hanging in the John Hopkins Halls today.

In November 1944, the first such operation took place on an extremely ill child. Alfred Blalock was the chief surgeon. He was surrounded by his assistants and nurses, as well as the crowded press corps, anxiously looking on. As Blalock was about to start the procedure, he demanded to know where Vivien Thomas was? Thomas was quickly ushered into the operating room, and a space was made for him, standing behind Blalock's right shoulder. Vivien Thomas advised Blalock throughout the operation. Soon the frail baby girl turned from a sickly blue to a healthy pink color. An ecstatic John Hopkins Hospital staff dubbed their tiny patient a 'miracle baby.' Medical history had been made that day. From then on, Vivien Thomas stood at Blalock's right shoulder during subsequent procedures.

During that first year at John Hopkins, about 200 procedures were performed on blue babies, with Vivien Thomas standing behind Blalock's right shoulder, as advisor. Not all operations were successful, but Blalock was persistent. In about two years, this procedure became close to routine.

Vivien Thomas had a knack for breaking down and explaining complicated procedures into simple steps. He performed his complicated procedures with no wasted motion. But in the late 1940's, Blalock and Thomas were far from co-equals. During the days, Thomas was training the next generation of heart specialist at John Hopkins. But during the evenings, Thomas had to moonlight as a bartender, often serving Blalock and the other white doctors he had been teaching earlier that day.

By the 1950's, this innovative surgery pioneered by Blalock, Taussig, Thomas had placed John Hopkins into the preeminent status it holds to this day. Alfred Blalock received the most, and well-deserved, accolades, including nomination several times for the Nobel Prize in Medicine. Of the three heart surgery pioneers, Vivien Thomas received little notoriety.

These three heart pioneers worked on the automatic implantable defibrillator, open-heart surgery, and heart transplants. In 1964, and less than three months after he retired from John Hopkins, Alfred Blalock died of cancer. Vivien Thomas, Blalock's partner for 34 years, remained at John Hopkins. It took Thomas some time to recover from Blalock's death. But Thomas eventually found his second calling; teaching and guiding the first generation of African American heart surgeons through the academic challenges at John Hopkins. For the next 15 years, Vivien Thomas mentored many future heart surgeons. Some became world famous.

In 1971, John Hopkins finally honored Vivien Thomas with a portrait hanging on a wall next to his medical peers. Thomas said he, "Felt quite humbled, but just a little bit proud." In 1976, John Hopkins honored Thomas with an 'Honorary Doctorate of Law.' It had to be law, because there is no such thing as an Honorary Doctorate of Medicine. In 1979, and after 37 years, that hard-working genius in the shadows, Vivien Thomas, retired from John Hopkins.

SOURCES:
Kalin, Andrea, and Duke, Bill *'American Experience: Partners of the Heart,'*
    DVD, PBS Home Video, 2003
Murphy, Jim, *'Breakthrough! –How Three People Saved 'Blue Babies,'*
    Clarion Books, New York, NY, 2015
Wyckoff, Edwin, *'The African-American Heart Surgery Pioneer –The Genius*
    of Vivien Thomas,' Enslow Publishers Inc., Berkeley Heights, NJ 2014

28

Jonas Salk (1914-1995)

... The Passionate Idealist Driven to Serve

Jonas Salk grew up in New York City, coming from a Russian-Jewish heritage. Jonas' heroes were Moses and Abraham Lincoln. In 1916, America's first polio (poliomyelitis) epidemic hit the country, afflicting 27,000, mostly children under the age of five. As a child, Jonas recalled seeing other young children afflicted by polio needing leg braces. New York City was especially hard hit with 2,400 deaths.[189]

As World War I was ending, young Jonas saw the numerous caskets of soldiers returning from the war, who were victims of the 1918 Spanish Flu. Every day, Jonas prayed he would do something good for mankind. He believed he could one day perform some noble service for humanity.[190]

In school, Jonas didn't especially stand-out, but as a student he had a quiet competence. Earlier medical researchers such as Louis Pasteur inspired him. At New York University Medical School, unlike many others in his classes, Jonas Salk gravitated towards research and laboratory work, rather than diagnosis treatments and the practice of medicine. But research lab work potential income was not as lucrative as practicing medicine. When a college professor told him he'd never become rich doing research, Jonas replied, "There is more in life than money." [191]

During his medical internship, Jonas was the ideal intern, and never complained about the lack sleep or tough schedules, and was held in high esteem by his fellow interns. He even stood up to a hospital administrator, who forbade interns from wearing a lapel button that stated 'Bundles for Britain,' an expression of support during World War II. Eventually, the administrator relented, and Jonas popularity among his peers rose further. Jonas' wife, Donna, called her husband a perfectionist, especially regarding laboratory work.

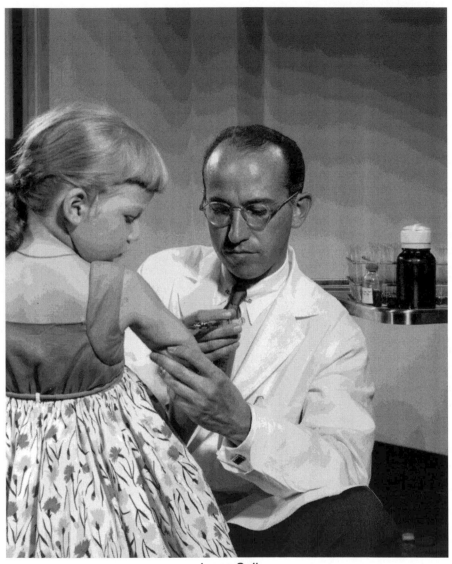

Jonas Salk

In medical school, Jonas came across a conundrum. A professor said in one class that a person could be immunized against the bacterial diseases tetanus or diphtheria by using toxins produced by these microbes after they were rendered harmless by chemicals. In a subsequent class, a professor said that developing immunity against viral diseases required an actual infection by a live virus. Salk pondered over this discrepancy, and soon found himself delving deeply into it.[192]

Salk set out to disprove the prevailing thought that only a live virus vaccine provided lifelong immunity against viral diseases. Live virus vaccines worked against smallpox, yellow fever and rabies. In 1942, most microbiologists believed any protective immunity conferred by a 'killed' virus vaccine would be short-lived, lasting no more than a few months. Jonas Salk thought otherwise.[193] When Salk relentlessly pursued his polio vaccine work, he used 'killed' polioviruses. This ran counter to the belief of many other preeminent virologists of the day.[194]

Earlier, in 1931, a doctor at the Rockefeller Institute proved that an unseen virus was the cause of influenza. It would take another decade, until the electron microscope was developed, before the actual viral structure could be seen by the human eye. One of those early virus pioneers was Doctor Thomas Francis Jr. When Jonas Salk was still in medical school, Francis became his mentor.

In 1942, Salk moved to Ann Arbor, Michigan. At the University of Michigan, Salk and Francis worked closely together for five years. The two researchers and their colleagues were attempting to develop a killed-virus vaccine against influenza. Their goal was to protect our troops fighting overseas in World War II. The first successful influenza vaccine was introduced in 1945.

Thomas Francis approached disease studies as an epidemiologist, while Salk approached these diseases as an immunologist.[195] An epidemiologist deals with a contagious disease that breaks out affecting the health of the population in a specific area. An immunologist inoculates against a contagious disease as a defense, should that disease become prevalent. Salk wanted to continue to work on improving vaccines, but he also wanted a greater degree of independence to work in his own manner. In 1947, Jonas Salk left Francis and the University of Michigan for a position with more autonomy at the University of Pittsburgh.

The National Foundation for Infantile Paralysis was best known for its fundraising program, the March of Dimes. The March of Dimes, a well known charity, approached Doctor Salk to help address the raging poliomyelitis issue. Polio had become an increasingly severe problem especially in more developed countries, where epidemics continued to grow in size and frequency. Children were consigned to the iron lung, young limbs withered, and death was a frequent visitor to nurseries.

The introduction of better sanitation, a generation or two earlier, had significantly reduced the incidence of diseases like cholera, dysentery and typhoid fever. However, better sanitation and hygiene had a downside with respect to the spread of poliomyelitis. Babies born in environments with poor hygiene were exposed to the poliovirus earlier in life. While these babies were still in the uterus, they had better protection from their mother's antibodies. After these babies were born, their mothers' breast milk continued to provide some degree of protection.[196] On the other hand, in communities with better sanitation, the polioviruses spread more readily. Babies would not be exposed in the very early stages life. Even an older child was more vulnerable because the mother's antibodies had worn off, and the child could become paralyzed by the viruses.

One of Salk's major challenges facing polio researchers was determining how many different types of poliovirus there were, so they all could be immunized against. Salk was chosen to head one of the teams working on this problem. The number of different poliovirus types turned out to be three.

Before long, Salk and the President of the March of Dimes, Basil O'Connor, became good friends. Basil O'Connor realized Salk had the skills and vision needed to tackle polio and create a vaccine. The March of Dimes provided continuing support for Salk's efforts.

By 1951, twenty-eight thousand polio cases wracked the country. In 1952, when the number of cases reached nearly 58,000, epidemiologists were forecasting one in eight families would have somebody stricken by polio. Salk and his team of skilled researchers experimented in laboratories and with monkeys. Salk knew, sooner or later, he'd have to do tests on children. Although Salk was confident of the experimental vaccine's safety, he confided to a reporter, "When you inoculate children with a polio vaccine for the first time, you don't sleep well for two or three weeks." [197]

Salk was always kind and personable, taking a special interest in as many children as possible. The head of one of his experimental inoculation schools found Dr. Salk extremely caring. This administrator decided he could trust Dr. Salk, because unlike so many other doctors, Dr. Salk took the time to write longhand legible letters in his correspondences.[198] Salk's early experiments on children were successful. The vaccine induced anti-polio antibodies with no negative side effects. This supported his hypothesis that an inactive <u>killed</u> virus might work rather than a potentially more dangerous <u>live</u> virus.[199] By 1953, Jonas Salk's success with the polio vaccine made him a household name.

By 1954, a national-wide field trial of the vaccine began. Two million children were involved. By 1955, successful statistical inferences were made public. The vaccine worked, and was declared 'safe, effective, and potent.' Salk never tried to make money from the vaccine. When television commentator Edward R. Murrow asked Dr. Salk and his co-researcher Dr. Thomas Francis, "Who held the patent on the vaccine?" Salk replied, "Well, the people, I would say. There is no patent. Could you patent the sun?" [200] After the TV interview, Murrow put his arm around Jonas' shoulders and said, "Young man, a great tragedy has just befallen you ...You have just lost your anonymity."

Since Jonas was quite young, he wanted to do something to benefit humanity. His wife, Donna, thought once he had accomplished this goal, he would return and be a family man. She was wrong. The Salk's family life would be forever changed, as the public wanted to anoint Jonas Salk as their national hero. Salk's ambition was to do great things for others, not to be considered great himself.

Some say Salk received too much credit for making the vaccine available to the public; others state the opposite. When President Eisenhower honored Salk at a ceremony in the White House Rose Garden, Salk responded, "When you single me out ...to receive this citation...you have been in similar situations, and I know that your thoughts were of the soldiers who crossed the Elbe [River] and not of yourself ...On behalf of all the people in the laboratories ...I gladly accept this recognition of what each of us has contributed." [201]

The success of the polio vaccine confirmed Salk's premise that a non-living vaccine protected against viral diseases. These successes have helped pave the way for additional non-living vaccines in years to come. Nevertheless, there were issues after the rollout of the vaccine. One of the six pharmaceutical companies that prepared the vaccine did not follow Dr. Salk's procedures. Consequently some children received an improperly made vaccine containing the live poliovirus, and contracted the disease. Salk's reputation was wrongly assailed. Salk explained, "Supposed you had a recipe for a cake, and every time you used that recipe, your cake turned out fine. Then you gave that same recipe to your neighbor. You didn't stay in the kitchen to see what she did, but her cake was terrible. Now, would you blame the recipe?" That pharmaceutical company's testing regulations were revised, and no safety issues with the vaccine have occurred since.

After he became a household name at 43 years old, Jonas Salk was uncertain where to go next. He was advised to do whatever made his heart leap. For Salk that meant solving problems that afflicted mankind. His dream was to bridge the huge gulf between the sciences and humanities.

Jonas Salk had long believed science and art went hand in hand, but now had grown too far apart. Salk believed that science and art could strengthen each other if brought closer together. To meld these two forces at one picturesque campus, he planned to attract some of the greatest scientific minds of the day. His chosen site would be an area of majestic natural beauty overlooking the Pacific Ocean.

In 1960, Dr. Salk founded the Salk Institute for Biological Studies outside San Diego. As its first director, Salk said, "We cannot be certain what will happen here, but we can be certain it will contribute to the welfare and understanding of man." The March of Dimes provided the initial funding with support from the National Institute of Health and other funding organizations. The Salk Institute researchers have addressed cancer, diabetes, birth defects, Alzheimer's disease, Parkinson's disease, AIDS, plant biology and more. The institute has given us new understanding and potential treatments for a range of diseases.

By the end of 1985, almost 23,000 Americans had contracted AIDS, and more than 11,000 had died. That was when Jonas Salk knew he again had to get personally involved. With his own laboratory at the Salk Institute now closed, he worked with others to create a vaccine against the virus that caused AIDS. This helped pave the way for future AIDS research.

In his last decades of life, Salk published four books dealing with humanity and its future. In one, *World Population and Human Values: A New Reality*, Salk states, "The well-being of people in other parts of the world is increasingly linked to our own, and our own, likewise, is increasing linked to theirs." In another book, *Anatomy of Reality*, Salk states, "We need to conduct ourselves so that our descendants will look back on us as having been good ancestors."

Some of his detractors have called his work kitchen chemistry, and likened him to a director of product development at a pharmaceutical company, making no true scientific discovery.[202] Others disagreed, pointing to major advances in human health that would not have occurred without Jonas Salk. In many ways, Salk did not behave like the typical academic scientist. However, there is no denying Jonas Salk made one of the most important contributions as one person. His contributions were enormous.[203] In an interview, a few years before he passed away, Salk expressed a humble conviction of God's power working through him.[204] Few can argue the world is not a better place because Jonas Salk, that idealist, wouldn't give up.

SOURCES:
Curson, Marjorie N., *Jonas Salk,*' Silver Burdett Press, Englewood Cliffs, NJ, 1990
Jacobs, Charlotte DeCroes, *Jonas Salk – A Life,*' Oxford University Press, New York, NY, 2015

John Wooden

29

John Wooden (1910-2010)

...Timeless Teacher and Coach

There are countless examples of outstanding teachers and coaches. Who can say, who are the best ones? Focusing on the sport of college basketball, one coach seems to stand ahead of others, UCLA's John Wooden.

John Wooden grew up in central Indiana's farmland. His father, Joshua, worked as a farmer and a postal carrier. Joshua Wooden never complained or had unkind words for others. Furthermore, Joshua instilled the idea of happiness and a sense of right and wrong in his four sons. Joshua told them a person's character was more important than his or her reputation. He advised his sons, "Never try to be better than somebody else, but also be the best you can be." In one very real sense, Joshua Wooden was a resounding success. All four of his sons became teachers.

Joshua's second son, John, also became a high school basketball star. After graduating, John Wooden starred at Indiana's Purdue University. He was nicknamed 'the Indiana Rubber Man,' because of his aggressive and speedy guard play, bouncing off the floors and spectators along the sidelines. As a player, John Wooden never had a technical foul. Later as a coach, he only had one called, for saying to a referee "Goodness Gracious, Sakes, Alive."

As a college basketball player in the early 1930's, John Wooden was recognized as the nation's best player. During his last two years at Purdue, John was also the team captain. In 1932, his senior year, he led his Purdue Boilermakers to the Big 10 as well as the NCAA Championship with a 17-1 record.

In 1932, when John Wooden graduated from Purdue, academically, he finished in the top 0.5 percent of his graduating class. Earlier, while in high school, John Wooden met his lifetime sweetheart, Nellie Riley. Soon after graduating from Purdue, John and Nellie were married in a small Indianapolis ceremony.

After their wedding, John and Nell Wooden departed Indiana for a high school teaching/coaching position in nearby Kentucky. After 11 years of high school basketball coaching, John Wooden had an 84 percent winning record. During World War II, John left high school coaching to join the U.S. Navy. He served nearly three years, and left the Navy as a Lieutenant. After the war, John accepted his fist college coaching assignment at Indiana State University. There he was also the athletic director as well as a teacher. At Indiana State, John completed his Masters Degree in education.

During his first year at Indiana State his team qualified for the post-season small college championship tournament. But when the tournament organizers informed him he would have to leave his one black player behind, John declined their invitation. The following year the rules changed; the color barrier was broken; and his team was again invited to this national tournament. Indiana State finished as the runner-ups. Small-time college coach John Wooden started to get noticed by larger institutions.

John Wooden always wanted to coach in his Big 10 Conference. Nell and he had hoped to remain in the Midwest. Purdue University, his ideal choice, wanted him. However, Purdue was slow and sloppy in handling the situation of the incumbent coach, a man John highly respected. The University of Minnesota tendered John an offer, but inclement winter weather delayed that offer's timely arrival. In the meantime, a head coaching offer from the UCLA Bruins arrived, and John accepted it. When the offer from the University of Minnesota later arrived, John could have chosen it, but stood by his commitment to UCLA. In 1948, John Wooden signed a three-year, $6,000 per year contract with UCLA. During his next 27 years at UCLA, he never asked for a raise, and he never made more than $35,000 per year. Several years before leaving UCLA, the owner of the professional Los Angeles Lakers Basketball team, Jack Kent Cooke, made John Wooden an exorbitant offer to coach the L.A. Lakers. John Wooden turned this and other offers down to remain in the college ranks with UCLA.

In 1964, and after 25 years as a college head coach, his UCLA college teams began an historic run. UCLA won 10 national championships in a period of twelve years, the latter twelve years of John's coaching career. During his time at UCLA, John Wooden was nicknamed 'the Wizard of Westwood,' a moniker he disdained for its immodesty.

How did coach and teacher John Wooden attain such a high level of success in his chosen profession? Here are a few possible insights: Besides his own father, his two favorite people were Abraham Lincoln and Mother Teresa of Calcutta. He told his players their education absolutely came first. Basketball, he said, came second because it paid their way through college with a scholarship. He also advised his players to get involved in other social activities, but he warned if these activities overtook education and basketball, his players might encounter issues.

John Wooden took his mantra from his college coach at Purdue: 'The team that makes the most mistakes will probably win, because if you're not making mistakes, you're not doing anything.' Wooden considered himself more of a practice coach, than a game strategy coach. He believed practicing was paramount, but he was not blind to the dangers of over-practicing and burn-out. John Wooden believed there were only two things detrimental to a player: (1) not reacting and (2) over-reacting. Likewise, he never wanted his players to feel winning was any great accomplishment, nor was losing anything to be ashamed of.

John Wooden listened to his individual players. He believed the surest way to show partiality was to treat everybody the same, because all players didn't earn or deserve the same treatment.

Wooden may have been the only basketball coach using ancient history to make points. He once told his players, "In history, all civilizations have crumbled from within, and the only thing that can possibly destroy this team is ourselves."

When his team won, as most often they did, he expected his players not to dance on the court and act like fools. When his team lost, he wanted no belly-aching. Dignity and perspective mattered above all. Wooden exhorted the UCLA fans not to be against their opponent but rather to be behind their UCLA team. He never used profanity. John Wooden strongly believed in prayer. All prayers were answered, he said, even though the answer often was a 'No.' But John did not believe in praying for victory in any basketball game. John Wooden believed true joy in life came from seeing the success of others.

Since 1977, the most outstanding men's college basketball player was chosen to receive the John Wooden Award. In 2004, that award was also extended to women's college basketball players. To be eligible for this prestigious award, a player must be a full-time student, have a cumulative grade point average of at least 2.0, have made outstanding contributions to team play, be a model citizen, and exhibit strength of character both on and off the basketball court.

John Wooden had perhaps hundreds of profound sayings that can be applied to the greater world outside of basketball. Here are a few of this author's favorites:

"I think the teaching profession contributes more to the future of our society than any other single profession."

"Young people need models, not critics."

"Pride is a better motivator than fear."

"If you're not making mistakes, then you're not doing anything. I'm positive that a doer makes mistakes."

"Be more concerned with your character than your reputation."

"Honors are fleeting, just as fame is; I cherish friendships more."

"Success is never final, failure is never fatal. It is courage that counts."

"Bad times can make you bitter OR better."

"Adversity is the state in which man most easily becomes acquainted with himself, being especially free of admirers then."

"Talent is God given. Be humble. Fame is man-given. Be grateful. Conceit is self-given. Be careful."

"If you're true to yourself, you're going to be true to everyone else."

"You can't live a perfect day without doing something for someone who will never be able to repay you."

"A man makes mistakes, but he isn't a failure until he starts blaming someone else."

"Don't let making a living prevent you from making a life."

\-

After her fight against cancer, John's wife, Nell, passed away on March 21, 1985. They had been sweethearts for 60 years, and married for almost 50 years. She was the only girl he ever went with. When Nell departed, John became a near recluse. Commemorating her passing, on the 21st of each month, a heart-broken John wrote a love letter to her. Then he'd place it in a stack with a yellow ribbon on her pillow of their bed. Eventually John overcame his depression, with the help of so many who loved him, his children, grandchildren, great-grandchildren, friends, and ex-players he had coached.

Before Nell died, John had a slight fear of death. After she passed away, he lost this fear. He believed a person who strove to become the best he or she could be, would stand tall on Judgment Day, regardless of whether or not that person accumulated possessions, fame, or power during their life. Late in his own life, John Wooden stated his greatest joy was seeing his players be successful in society, especially in non-basketball pursuits. He delighted in knowing what nearly all of the 180 players whom he coached were doing in today's world. Many of his players acknowledge John Wooden just didn't teach them basketball; he taught them 'Life!'

\-

SOURCE:
Johnson, Neville L, *The John Wooden Pyramid of Success, 2nd Edition,'*
    Cool Titles, Los Angeles, CA, 2003

Arland Williams

30

Arland D. Williams Jr. (1935-1982)

... The Ultimate Sacrifice for Desperate Strangers

This author remembers the day well, in his old hometown of Washington, D.C. There was a subway accident in the Metro Rail system where three people died and 25 were injured. But the biggest news on Wednesday January 13th, 1982, was happening three miles away. Upon taking off from Washington's National Airport, Air Florida Flight 90 crashed into the Potomac River with 79 passengers and crew. The improperly de-iced Boeing 737 stuck one of the three roadway spans of the 14th Street Bridges, the Rochambeau Bridge, and destroyed seven vehicles, causing four motorist fatalities on the bridge, before the plane plunged into the frozen river 200 feet from shore.

Over the years, we have occasionally heard of a parent sacrificing their life to protect their child, using their own body as a shield against falling earthquake rubble, or something similar. Think of the soldier sacrificing his life by jumping onto a live grenade to save nearby buddies. Some of those buddies were probably great friends, others were just buddies, while others were likely tolerable, just as in about any human group situation. But one seldom hears of a person sacrificing him or herself for strangers, albeit these strangers were all in the same precarious bind. Air Florida 90 passenger Arland Williams did just that in January 1982.

Earlier that fateful morning, a storm that produced six inches of snow had closed National Airport. About noon, the airport reopened as the snowfall slackened. Conditions were treacherous, but the airport had often operated in worse conditions. At about 1:45 PM, the airplane that became Air Florida Flight 90 landed at National Airport. This flight departed from Miami two hours and forty-five minutes earlier. Later that afternoon, this plane was supposed to return to Florida via Tampa and Fort Lauderdale.

Arland William was a veteran bank examiner, from a small town in Illinois. He was on a short business trip to Washington to recommend to those in charge that a failing bank in Florida ought to be shut down. This was during the early stages of our nation's great Savings and Loan debacle of the 1980's. The major component of that financial crisis was recent federal deregulation.

Like most passengers in those days, Arland Williams probably boarded Air Florida Flight 90, maybe forty minutes before the scheduled gate departure time. Perhaps Arland had a chance to chat with a few fellow passengers? Maybe not. After the loaded plane departed from the gate, it had to wait for another 49 minutes, due to the take-off backlog caused by the foul weather.

Unknown to the passengers, the plane's wings had not been properly de-iced, as light snow continued falling. The pilot should have known better. If he was atop matters, he would have delayed his already behind schedule take-off even longer, and returned his plane to the terminal for another reapplication of de-icing. But he didn't. He tried to take-off from the longest runway after rolling a half-mile longer than usual. Air Florida 90 had not attained enough speed to safely lift from the ground. Indeed, the plane barely attained enough speed to get airborne. Once airborne, the ice build-up on the wings greatly compromised the plane's performance. Air Florida 90 never got higher than a few hundred feet, and remained in the sky for only about 30 seconds. The plane had traveled about one mile in the air, before it stalled and crashed into the 14th Street Bridge over the Potomac River. Air Florida 90 broke apart.

Near the tail section, six people, five passengers and one flight attendant, survived the initial impact, and were able to extricate themselves from the wreckage. These six survivors found themselves disoriented, most were injured, but all were alive and floating or hanging on to the tail section in the icy river.

About 20 minutes after Air Florida 90 crashed, a two-man National Park Police helicopter arrived on the scene. The hovering craft dangled a lifeline, and on later attempts dipped its skids into the treacherous river, attempting to retrieve exhausted survivors. The injured survivors, whose scant strength was being sapped by the icy water, could only be dragged to the shore, one at a time. Three times, when the helicopter returned to the wreckage, Arland Williams passed off the lifeline or offered the helicopter skid to a fellow survivor. When the helicopter returned to the wreckage site to pick up their last man, Arland William's body had given out. He was gone.

Arland Williams was not the only hero after the crash. The two men in the Park Police helicopter risked their craft, and their lives, by successfully making dangerous maneuvers to save people, one by one, from the water. One of those survivors in the water didn't have enough strength to maintain her grip onto the life ring dangling from the helicopter. On the river bank, a returning home federal employee, Lenny Skutnik, saw what was happening. Skutnik didn't need to think twice. He immediately striped off his coat and boots, jumped into the icy river and swam out about 30 feet to the weakened woman and rescued her.

Almost two weeks after the accident, Roger Rosenblatt of Time Magazine wrote about Arland Williams, "He could not make ice storms, or freeze the water until it froze the blood. But he could hand life over to a stranger, and that is a power of nature too. The man in the water pitted himself against an implacable, impersonal enemy; he fought it with charity; and he held it to a standoff. He was the best we can do." [205]

Three years later, that bridge span was renamed, the 'Arland D. Williams Jr. Memorial Bridge.' His alma mater, the Citadel in Charleston, South Carolina, started the 'Arland D. Williams, Jr. Society' to honor students who performed distinguished community service.

SOURCES:
The Weather Channel, *Why Planes Crash,--Jet Crashes into Icy River*
Time Magazine, January 25, 1982
Washington Post Newspaper, January 14, 1982

31

The New York City Police and Firefighters (-- 2001)

...Just Doing Their Job

The dawn over New York City on Tuesday September 11, 2001 heralded a cloudless azure sky. Highly professional city firefighters and policemen awoke, dressed, and set out for another day of 'just doing their job' ...serving the public.

We were all shocked witnessing the explosions, the collapsing Twin Towers and the unimaginable death and destruction. Yet our First Responders reactions were immediate and professional. They trained hard and often rehearsed for many anticipated possible contingencies. Yet, this 'mother of them all,' caught them all by surprise. By nightfall, thousands never made it home to their families that horrible evening.

Tuesday, September 11, 2001 stirs our emotions as few other days have. We saw the worst and the best in our human nature. We had to acknowledge that we were hated, this time by Muslim extremists. We encountered new phenomenon in our society, some of it good and some of it less so: tighter security at airports and other public places, less tolerance for certain religions, and talk of isolationism. This author can't help but recall a caution espoused by founding father, Benjamin Franklin, "They that can give up essential liberty [freedom] to obtain a little temporary safety [security] deserve neither liberty nor safety." Franklin's warning, taken with obvious practical cautions and reasonable measures, should resonate.

On that beautiful September day, 2,977 people in America, coming from more than 90 different countries, were murdered by Muslim extremists. Victims perished in New York City, at the U.S. Pentagon and aboard United Airlines Flight 93. It was the deadliest attack ever on American soil. It rivaled Pearl Harbor 60 years earlier. In times like those, we saw the worst in our human nature. However, as President Lincoln stated, 'the Better Angels in our Nature' also became evident. Those 'Better Angels' were manifested in the selfless acts and countless deeds known only to God.

Many American heroes gave us their very best, the everyday passengers aboard United Airlines Flight 93, and first responders at the U.S. Pentagon and in New York City. The New York Volunteer Fire Department lost 343 firefighters, and the New York Police Department lost 72 officers. These public servants were simply doing their job that fateful late summer day. They were the best in us.

SOURCES:
Various

ACKNOWLEDGEMENTS

A book like this needs many sources and a handful of reviewers.

I've probably read over a hundred books and watched or listened to hundreds of hours of DVDs before putting pen to paper. While it's impossible to include every source of insight, many are acknowledged at the end of each of the 31 chapters.

Several outstanding sources inspired me to look more deeply into our American History: Anything researched and written by David McCullough, Doris Kearns-Goodwin or Stephen Ambrose always prompts me to look further. Likewise, I strongly believe filmmaker Ken Burns and his staff at Florentine Films research and produce the best programming on television. I was concerned when I learn of our 45th U.S. President's plan to privatize the Corporation for Public Broadcasting and eliminate the National Endowment for Arts and the Humanities. Americans sorely need more such education, especially in history, so we are less inclined to repeat the sweeping mistakes we have made in our past.

Research and work by the likes of McCullough, Kearns-Goodwin, Ambrose, Burns and many others will hopefully continue to edify all Americans. These well known researchers and historians have influenced my own personal desire to research and to learn more about our shared American Experience.

Others, less well-known, aided me in this project. International Trade Specialist Ralph Watkins of Eugene, Oregon, was most helpful refining several sections of this book. Likewise, Mark Durham and William E. 'Stitch,' Wilson, both of Morgantown, West Virginia improved sections of this book. Arriving at a title for this work took well over a year. Here, my brother Keith, of Melbourne Beach, Florida, had an inspired idea.

Fred Myers of Florence, Alabama contributed many careful suggestions, as well offered some sound advice for the Author's Notes and refining the title. Ron Stob of Highlands Ranch, Colorado offered a handful of astute editorial improvements. Cathy Casteleiro of Crystal Beach, Florida did extraordinary work producing this book's cover and refining the interior images. She was also extremely helpful with final book formatting. Coming up with the 48 portraits or photographs that enhanced this book was a challenge. In this regard, Jeff Bridgers at the Library of Congress and Erin Beasley at the Smithsonian Institution's National Portrait Gallery were immensely helpful. Many a Friday night,

Emil Pastor, a building contractor in St. Petersburg, Florida would join me for a beer, to share our past week's happenings. For a year and half, Emil took a genuine interest in this project, and offered countless helpful suggestions.

Ruth Liss, the former Editor of the International Forest Products Association Transport Association Journal in Brussels, Belgium, was invaluable. I've dealt with many editors for my previous nine books, but never have I dealt with one as professional and as conscientious, or one who has improved a book the way Ruth has. What else can I say about Ruth?

DEDICATION

Ruth Liss and I share past common interests in forest products, marine shipping, writing, and public speaking. We met at a Toastmasters Club in St. Petersburg, Florida. Her goal, she said laughingly, was to keep her gray matter in the pink. I was her mentor.

Ruth was a school teacher in inner city Newark, New Jersey, a magazine editor and an interviewer in Europe, and enjoyed being mother to a little boy. Ruth's husband of 34 years passed away suddenly on a tennis court in Brussels, Belgium. Ruth then returned to the U.S. to start life anew.

After mid-life Peace Corps volunteering, I needed many knee surgeries. Following that sixth knee surgery, and again not totally successful, there was Ruth, upbeat as ever, and always supportive. There were times during this project when I was discouraged, trying to plow-through some source book that was difficult to grasp. Nevertheless, always cheerful Ruth inspired me to keep moving forward. Aside from being the chief editor of this project, countless times Ruth provided me with invaluable advice while I was in the throes of researching, writing, and organizing this work.

THIS BOOK IS DEDICATED TO MY DEAREST FRIEND,
RUTH ELIZABETH LISS

Other Non-Fiction Books by Captain Rick Rhodes:

The Ohio River – Voyaging on Today's River, Heron Island Guides,
St. Petersburg, FL, 2010
The Ohio River – In American History (Hardcover), Heron Island Guides,
St. Petersburg, FL, 2008
The Ohio River – In American History and Voyaging on Today's River,
Heron Island Guides, St. Petersburg, FL, 2007
Discovering the Tidal Potomac – A Cruising Guide & Boating Ref., 2nd Ed.,
Heron Island Guides, 2003
Cruising Guide to Florida's Big Bend – Including the Apalachicola, Chattahoochee,
Flint, and Suwannee Rivers, Pelican Publishing Company, New Orleans, LA, 2003
Cruising Guide from Lake Michigan to Kentucky Lake – The Heartland Rivers Route,
Pelican Publishing Company, New Orleans, LA, 2002
Honduras and its Bay Islands – A Mariner's Guide, Heron Island Guides, 1998
Discovering the Tidal Potomac – A Cruising Guide & Boating Ref., 1st Ed.,
Heron Island Guides, 1998
Cruising Guide to the Bay Island of Honduras, Wescott Cove Publishing Company,
Stamford, CT, 1996

Rick Rhodes
360 Mt. Oak Ave, NE
St. Petersburg, FL. 33702
Fax: 727-527-8287
Website:
www.heronislandguides.com

206

INDEX

ENDNOTES

[1] The National Portrait Gallery is part of the Smithsonian Institute in Washington DC

[2] Fleming, Thomas, *'Ben Franklin –Inventing America,'* page 193

[3] Fleming, page 10

[4] Fleming, page 20

[5] Fleming, page 60

[6] Fleming, page 50

[7] Harrison, Lowell H., *'George Rogers Clark and the War in the West,'* page 4

[8] Harrison, page 109

[9] DeLeeuw, Adele, *'George Rogers Clark –Frontier Fighter,'* page 12

[10] Harrison, page 14

[11] Lee, Susan and John, *'George Rogers Clark: War in West,'* page 5

[12] Harrison, page 60

[13] Harrison, page 85

[14] Harrison, page 100

[15] Harrison, page 107

[16] McCraw, Thomas K, *'The Founders and Finance,'* page 189

[17] Walters, Raymond, Jr. *'Albert Gallatin,'* page vi

[18] Walters, page 4

[19] McCraw, page 321

[20] McCraw, page 210

[21] Walters, page 214

[22] McCraw, page 205

[23] Walters, page 262

[24] Walters, page 141

[25] McCraw, page 228

[26] Walters, page 170

[27] McCraw, page 276

[28] McCraw, page 282

[29] McCraw, page 285

[30] McCraw, page 181

[31] McCraw, page 296

[32] Walters, page 316

[33] McCraw, page 320

[34] McCraw, page 321

[35] McCraw, page 323

[36] McCraw, page 326

[37] Danisi, page 81

[38] Ambrose, Stephen E., *'Undaunted Courage,'* page 91

[39] Danisi, page 315

[40] Danisi, page 335

[41] Danisi, page 272

[42] Gronenman III, William, *'David Crockett –Hero of the Common Man,'* page 31

[43] Gronenman, page 99

[44] Gronenman, page 148

[45] Kennedy, John Fitzgerald, *Profiles in Courage,* page 62

[46] A latitude line 49 degrees north and parallel to the equator. Each line of latitude is 60 nautical miles.

[47] Sherlock, Vivian M, *The Fever Man, A Biography of Dr. John Gorrie,* page 3

[48] Sherlock, page 56

[49] Sherlock, page 76

[50] Sherlock, page 100

[51] Sherlock, page 61

[52] Sherlock, page 117

[53] Sherlock, page 127

[54] Clinton, Catherine, *Harriet Tubman,* page 18

[55] Stiehm, Jamie, *Parallel Lives from the Eastern Shore,* New York Times, June 24, 2011

[56] Becker, Helaine, *Frederick Douglass,* page 21

[57] Becker, page 8

[58] Becker, page 30

[59] Becker, page 39

[60] Becker, page 53

[61] Becker, page 69

[62] Becker, page 74

[63] Becker, page 84

[64] Squier, Robert, *Who Was Frederick Douglass,* page 91

[65] Squier, page 95

[66] Taylor, page 9

[67] Taylor, page 307

[68] Taylor, page 305

[69] Taylor, page 298

[70] Taylor, page 227

[71] Taylor, John M., *William Henry Seward, Lincoln's Right Hand,* page 66

[72] Taylor, page 256

[73] Taylor, page 292

[74] Taylor, page 191

[75] Taylor, page 240

[76] Taylor, page 282

[77] Taylor, page 275

[78] Taylor, page 306

[79] Taylor, page 296

[80] Ashby, Ruth, *Extraordinary People,* page 12

[81] Smith, Diane Monroe, *Fanny and Joshua,* page 18

[82] Krensky, Stephen, *Clara Barton Biography,* page 67

[83] Krensky, page 90

[84] Krensky, page 115

[85] Krensky, page 117

[86] Karabell, Zachary, *'Chester Alan Arthur,'* page 29

[87] Karabell, page 94

[88] Otfinoski, Steven, *'Chester Arthur,'* page 94

[89] Otfinoski, page 93

[90] Karabell, page 90

[91] Karabell, page 143

[92] Outman, James, *'Industrial Revolution Biographies,'* page 71

[93] Outman, page 70

[94] Carey, Charles W Jr., *'George Washington Carver,'* page 22

[95] Carey, page 30

[96] Carey, page 33

[97] Bureau of Transportation Statistics U.S. Department of Transportation

[98] McCullough, David, *'The Wright Brothers,'* page 17

[99] McCullough, page 32

[100] McCullough, page 50

[101] McCullough, page 98

[102] McCullough, page 75

[103] McCullough, page 102

[104] McCullough, page 141

[105] McCullough, page 203

[106] McCullough, page 222

[107] McCullough, page 226

[108] McCullough, page 340

[109] McCullough, page 354

[110] McCullough, page 417

[111] McCullough, page 447

[112] McCullough, page 448

[113] McCullough, page 452

[114] McCullough, page 457

[115] McCullough, page 463

[116] McCullough, page 463

[117] A league 'Triple Crown' is not awarded every year. It's awarded rarely, and when a player can lead his league in home runs, batting average, plus runs-batted-in (RBI's).

[118] Greenberger, Robert, *'Lou Gehrig,'* page 21

[119] Buckley, James, Jr, *'Lou Gehrig: Iron Horse of Baseball,'* page 32

[120] Greenberger, page 5

[121] Buckley, page 59

[122] Buckley, page 85

[123] Greenberger, page 76

[124] Greenberger, page 90

[125] Buckley, page 88

[126] Greenberger, page 92

[127] Ward and Burns, *'Baseball –The American Epic –Shadow Ball,'* page 32

[128] Posnanski, Joe, *'The Soul of Baseball…'* page 178

[129] Posnanski, page 189

[130] Ward and Burns, page 15

[131] Ward and Burns, page 54

[132] Posnanski, page 6

[133] Posnanski, page 12

[134] Posnanski, page 57

[135] Posnanski, page 202

[136] Posnanski, page 153

[137] Ward and Burns, page 71

[138] Burns and Novick, *'Baseball,'* DVD #9

[139] Posnanski, page 35

[140] Posnanski, page 81

[141] Posnanski, page 84

[142] Posnanski, page 94

[143] Posnanski, page 190

[144] Reda, Lou, *'Great Commanders —George C. Marshall: Soldier and Statesman,'*

[145] McCullough, David, *'Truman,'* page 798

[146] McCullough, page 558

[147] McCullough, David, *'Truman,'* page 990

[148] Mara, Wil, *'Harry Truman —Presidents and Their Times,'* page 10

[149] Schuman, Michael A. *'Harry S. Truman,'* page 29

[150] Mara, page 6

[151] Mara, page 29

[152] Schuman, page 33

[153] Schuman, page 36

[154] Mara, page 33

[155] Schuman, page 39

[156] Schuman, page 42

[157] Mara, page 42

[158] Mara, page 44

[159] Mara, page 49

[160] McCullough, page 320

[161] McCullough, page 353

[162] McCullough, page 731

[163] McCullough, page 585

[164] Schuman, page 54

[165] Schuman, page 56

[166] Schuman, page 56

[167] Mara, page 65

[168] Schuman, page 61

[169] Mara, page 69

[170] McCullough, page 597

[171] Mara, page 78

[172] Schuman, page 87
[173] McCullough, page 860
[174] McCullough, page 915
[175] McCullough, page 949
[176] Mara, page 91
[177] McCullough, page 957
[178] McCullough, page 525
[179] McCullough, page 991
[180] McCullough, page 992
[181] Schuman, page 100
[182] McCullough, page 989
[183] Mara, page 96
[184] Law, Steven, 'The Last Plains Indian War Chief ...'
[185] Law, Steven, 'The Last Plains Indian War Chief ...'
[186] Law, Steven, 'The Last Plains Indian War Chief ...'
[187] Law, Steven, 'The Last Plains Indian War Chief ...'
[188] Law, Steven, 'The Last Plains Indian War Chief ...'
[189] Jacobs, Charlotte DeCroes, 'Jonas Salk –A Life,' page 3
[190] Jacobs, page 15
[191] Jacobs, page 21
[192] Jacobs, page 24
[193] Jacobs, page 46
[194] Jacobs, page 101
[195] Jacobs, page 51
[196] Jacobs, page 74
[197] Jacobs, page 109
[198] Jacobs, page 110
[199] Jacobs, page 111
[200] Curson, Marjorie N., 'Jonas Salk,' page 97
[201] Jacobs, page 176
[202] Jacobs, page 456
[203] Jacobs, page 457
[204] Jacobs, page 451
[205] Rosenblatt, Roger 'Time Magazine,' January 25, 1982